D0233484

An Integrated Approach to
Family Work for Psychosis

of related interest

Conduct Disorder and Offending Behaviour in Young People
Findings from Research
Kristin Liabø and Joanna Richardson
ISBN 978 1 84310 508 4

Cannabis and Young People
Reviewing the Evidence
Richard Jenkins
ISBN 978 1 84310 398 1

The Madness of Our Lives
Experiences of Mental Breakdown and Recovery
Penny Gray
Foreword by Peter Campbell
ISBN 978 1 84310 057 7

A Multidisciplinary Handbook of Child and Adolescent Mental Health for Front-line Professionals
Nisha Dogra, Andrew Parkin, Fiona Gale and Clay Frake
Foreword by Panos Vostanis
ISBN 978 1 85302 929 5

Choosing a Groupwork Approach
An Inclusive Stance
Oded Manor
ISBN 978 1 85302 870 0

Mental Health and Social Work
Edited by Marion Ulas and Anne Connor
ISBN 978 1 85302 302 6

Introducing Mental Health
A Practical Guide
Caroline Kinsella and Connor Kinsella
Foreword by Vikram Patel
ISBN 978 1 84310 260 1

Psychosis
Understanding and Treatment
Edited by Jane Ellwood
ISBN 978 1 85302 265 4

Group Psychotherapy of the Psychoses
Concepts, Interventions and Contexts
Edited by Victor L. Schermer and Malcolm Pines
Foreword by Howard Kibel
ISBN 978 1 85302 584 6

Beyond Madness
Psychosocial Interventions in Psychosis
Edited by Joseph H. Berke, Margaret Fagan, George Mak-Pearce and Stella Pierides-Müller
ISBN 978 1 85302 889 2

An Integrated Approach To Family Work For Psychosis

A Manual for Family Workers

Gina Smith, Karl Gregory and Annie Higgs

Jessica Kingsley Publishers
London and Philadelphia

First published in 2007
by Jessica Kingsley Publishers
116 Pentonville Road
London N1 9JB, UK
and
400 Market Street, Suite 400
Philadelphia, PA 19106, USA

www.jkp.com

Copyright © Gina Smith, Karl Gregory and Annie Higgs 2007

The right of Gina Smith, Karl Gregory and Annie Higgs to be identified as authors of this work has been asserted by them in accordance with the Copyright, Designs and Patents Act 1988.

All rights reserved. No part of this publication may be reproduced in any material form (including photocopying or storing it in any medium by electronic means and whether or not transiently or incidentally to some other use of this publication) without the written permission of the copyright owner except in accordance with the provisions of the Copyright, Designs and Patents Act 1988 or under the terms of a licence issued by the Copyright Licensing Agency Ltd, 90 Tottenham Court Road, London, England W1T 4LP. Applications for the copyright owner's written permission to reproduce any part of this publication should be addressed to the publisher.

Warning: The doing of an unauthorised act in relation to a copyright work may result in both a civil claim for damages and criminal prosecution.

Library of Congress Cataloging in Publication Data
Smith, Gina, 1957-
    An integrated approach to family work for psychosis : a manual for family workers / Gina Smith, Karl Gregory, and Annie Higgs.
        p. ; cm.
    Includes bibliographical references and index.
    ISBN-13: 978-1-84310-369-1 (pb)
    ISBN-10: 1-84310-369-9 (pb)
    1. Psychoses--Treatment. 2. Psychoses--Patients--Family relationships. 3. Family social work. 4. Family therapy. I. Gregory, Karl. II. Higgs, Annie, 1959- III. Title.
    [DNLM: 1. Psychotic Disorders--therapy. 2. Caregivers--psychology. 3. Family--psychology. 4. Family Therapy--methods. 5. Professional-Family Relations. WM 200 S648i 2007]
    RC512.S57 2007
    362.2'6--dc22

2006037490

British Library Cataloguing in Publication Data
A CIP catalogue record for this book is available from the British Library

ISBN 978 1 84310 369 1

Printed and bound in Great Britain by
Athenaeum Press, Gateshead, Tyne and Wear

UNIVERSITY OF PLYMOUTH

9007547696

Contents

WITHDRAWN
FROM
UNIVERSITY OF PLYMOUTH
LIBRARY SERVICES

Section 2: Delivering Family Work for Psychosis

Foreword

Fifty years ago pioneering research by George Brown on the concept of expressed emotion changed the way in which people with schizophrenia and their families were treated. Crucially this work, which stimulated an impressive array of studies, models of intervention and training programmes, has still not been widely adopted clinically.

For those who embrace family inclusion as a fundamental philosophy this lack of uptake is really perplexing. Indeed, after completing the training with Professor Julian Leff, I worked with numerous families as our team wholeheartedly believed in the pragmatic approach and we went out of our way to make it possible. So when I was offered the opportunity to become a trainer in 1991, I questioned the post's long term viability; surely the role would rapidly become superfluous as there would be immediate universal uptake! This proved not to be the case. Whilst the intervention is efficacious, the attitudes and beliefs towards its necessity and timing fall along a highly variable continuum. Reasons for this are multifaceted: historically rigid service styles, other responsibilities and lack of supervision, reportedly prevent those trained in family intervention from using their skills routinely (Fadden 1997).

Clearly Gina Smith, Karl Gregory and Annie Higgs have considered the prevailing evidence. Over the last decade, by combining tenacity with high levels of motivation, they, despite meeting implementation obstacles, have quietly got on with establishing a nationally recognised family intervention service. Their strategy has been fourfold: securing funding to develop champions; establishing robust training packages; ensuring those trained are supported to use the approach and finally getting family work on their Trust board's strategic agenda (see preface). This has helped to ensure that carers have been involved at every level and their perspective is clearly woven throughout the book. Drawing on their knowledge and experience, these compassionate leaders in the field of family work implementation encapsulate the lessons learnt from those they have worked with.

In constructing a twenty-first century family work manual I am struck by the fact Gina, Karl and Annie haven't thrown the baby out with bath water. There is much value in respecting our forefathers' work, understanding the theory and taking steps to appreciate how different family intervention models were created.

The manner in which the manual and its chapters are set out demonstrate an adherence to the evidence base. A repertoire of skills and knowledge is advocated by overtly demonstrating how models and theories can be synthesised to suit the needs of every family system. What is known to be effective has not been abandoned, but the notion of every problem being treated like a nail when you are only equipped with a hammer is. Today's families come from diverse cultures, so one model does not fit all. To tailor make packages of care, contemporary practice demands flexibility.

Translating the research into clinical ingredients provides a useful set of workable recipes, which fifty years on with continued perseverance will contribute in helping clinicians and their managers to implement the approach.

The book is going in my tool box.

Catherine Gamble BA(Hons), RGN, RMN, RNT, Consultant Nurse, South West London and St George's Mental Health Care Trust, London; Co-editor of Working With Serious Mental Illness: A Manual for Clinical Practice 2nd edition

Reference:
Fadden, G. (1997) 'Implementation of family interventions in routine clinical practice following staff training programmes: a major cause for concern', *Journal of Mental Health 6*, 6 599–612

Preface

Family work is essentially practical in its focus. The principles captured within this manual have emerged from our own experience of working with scores of families, as well as that derived 'second-hand' through training and supervising dozens of family workers.

Our integrated family work model has been enthusiastically adopted by practitioners in a broad range of settings. They report its applicability and utility in practice with families that they have joined in their journeys of recovery. We hope that those using this manual will appreciate that it is not just about 'doing family work' but rather 'being with families'.

We recommend that family work should not be seen as a specialist intervention, but that it becomes recognised as part of routine practice, delivered by mental health workers who have undertaken some additional training. This training may be gained through attending a formal course or by working as an apprentice to an experienced family worker. All family workers can give and receive support in practice through peer supervision. It is also beneficial to have access to a worker who has developed a strong knowledge of the theory underpinning family interventions, to help consider alternative strategies when working with complex situations.

Our work with families across three counties has given us the opportunity to work within two mental health care trusts: the Avon and Wiltshire Mental Health Partnership NHS Trust (AWP) and the Gloucestershire Partnership Trust (GPT). These two organisations have chosen to support the implementation of family work for psychosis in somewhat different ways.

- In 1998 AWP invested in a year-long funded development project, which resulted in a successful strategy for delivering family interventions across the whole organisation, without the need for a specialist service (DH 1999). The key to this strategy is a funded family work champion post (Smith and Velleman 2002) to ensure there are sufficient family workers in all localities and to maintain the focus on family interventions when other service pressures threaten this.

- GPT adopted an alternative stance, investing more broadly in all psychosocial interventions (not singling out family work for psychosis) through its development of a local Thorn Course (Baguley *et al.* 2000), which happily mental health workers from AWP can now access too. GPT therefore has a significant number of trained family workers, but we notice without a family work champion the routine availability of family interventions is less clear than in AWP. Despite there being no particular coordination, the tenacity and continuing ability to be the holders of hope for change exhibited by many Thorn-trained practitioners and several senior managers continue to keep family work on the Trust's strategic agenda. Together they are striving to see this work as an integral part of GPT in-patient and community services.

Both GPT and AWP have developed family interventions to suit the needs of families during a service user's in-patient treatment. These successful initiatives have already been presented at a number of conferences and will soon appear in peer-reviewed journals.

Whatever framework services use to assess, plan, implement and evaluate the care provided – which for services operating in England will be the Care Programme Approach, as demanded by the National Service Framework for Mental Health (DH 1999) – it should state that family interventions are taking place, to ensure that the work with the family is reviewed as part of the whole package of care. Family intervention is likely to appear on a care plan to meet a carer's needs as well as that of the service user.

We wanted to call this manual *Family Work for Psychosis: The Next Generation*; however, our publishers felt an obviously descriptive title was more appropriate, or maybe they just aren't *Star Trek* fans. Either way, we bowed to their better judgement. Nonetheless, we feel it right to make reference to the next generation for family work. We had the first-generation studies that gave us the research findings (Lam 1991; Mari and Streiner 1994) on which to base our practice, and the second-generation studies (Fadden 1998) that strengthened and refined our knowledge of what works in practice. We now know with some certainty that family work for psychosis is effective on a number of levels, yet it remains hard to offer in routine practice. We hope, through the practice guidance proffered within this manual, that the next generation of families coping with psychosis will all be well served through the regular provision of family work.

Authors' note

It is tempting when writing a manual such as this to feel compelled to respond to every new policy initiative that overlaps the sphere of interest. Indeed, we found it hard to draw a line, but ultimately felt we must if we were ever going to get this manual to press. We therefore acknowledge that we have not, for example, explored the distinct concerns of women coping with psychosis, or discussed the growing evidence base (rather than merely good practice guidelines) for working with first-episode psychosis. We plan to address these issues with some rigour in future published work.

Acknowledgements

First, we would like to thank all the families coping with psychosis and other mental illnesses we have worked with over many years. We thank them for what they have taught us, and for their encouragement as we have developed and refined our practice. We also thank them for the great generosity they have shown to others, despite their own struggles.

In particular we thank Lu Duhig, an extremely resourceful carer for her son who has grappled with schizophrenia for some time; she works closely with Gina in the Avon and Wiltshire Mental Health Partnership NHS Trust (AWP). We have drawn on the information she has produced for carers (in the form of an accessible resource pack that is available in paper format to all carers in the AWP catchment area and to others via the website: www.carershelpcarers.org.uk) to help us define the carer's role and empathise with the challenges she or he faces.

We thank our students and supervisees, who have been keen to share our knowledge and skill, to learn from us in order to develop their family work practice. It was really they who led us to write this manual, to formalise what we have found to work and to share it more widely.

Our special thanks go also to Catherine Gregory. Latterly we have benefited from her computer skills as she formatted the manuscript for us before sending it to the publishers, but more importantly we remember her input in the early days, when we were unused to writing together and agonised over the right words to use to convey our meaning. Her knowledge of the English language stopped us agonising too long and prevented us from getting stuck! She has also been willing to listen to our ideas; as someone who is neither a practitioner nor steeped in family work she has been able to help us to try to ensure that our words make sense and avoid the use of jargon anywhere in the manual.

We also offer our thanks to Rachel Perkins, although she probably does not realise she helped us. However, in a recent conversation with Gina she mentioned the importance of reading the text aloud when preparing an article or book for publication. Having adopted this suggestion, we realise the great value of this advice (which we encourage others to follow in their writing), as it quickly reveals convoluted sentences that need to be simplified. We hope, as you read this manual, you will find it as easy to follow as we intend it to be.

Departing from tradition we would also like to acknowledge each other as authors of this manual. It has always been a venture in which we have worked as equals, with no one taking more credit than the others and each of us offering his or her own knowledge and skills drawn from wide-ranging experience. Through this endeavour we have come to really appreciate each other in a way that will endure long after the manual appears in print.

The manual has taken us over three years to write, because we have been beset by an unusual number of major life events, including births, life-threatening illnesses and sadly several deaths too. Happily at any time one of us was willing and able to take over the lead, providing support and direction to the other two at crucial moments. As we have come through these impediments we have developed very strong working relationships, without which this manual probably would never have materialised and would have remained just a 'good idea'. Throughout this whole process we have really appreciated the support we have received from Jessica Kingsley Publishers, for the space they gave us when we needed it, alongside their ongoing gentle encouragement and advice.

Finally, we would like to thank our own families, for their love and support, as they have encouraged us to write this book, even at times when it has taken us away from spending time with them. We send them all our love.

Section 1

Understanding Family Work for Psychosis

1

Introduction

How to use this manual

In this manual we aim to present clear strategies for engaging with carers alongside people who experience psychosis, to reduce the risk of relapse and improve the quality of life for all concerned. Some guidance is also offered, drawn from our experiences, to help workers new to this area explore (and adapt where necessary) the practices within their workplace in order to fit family interventions in to their work routine.

In Section 1 of the manual we have adopted a layout that we think is logical, following the guidance of Kipling's 'six honest serving-men' (Kipling 2000, p.72), whom he claimed taught him all he knew; he gave these men the names What, Why, When, Who, Where and How. Consequently, we discuss the various components of family work in the following way: what is family work, why is it offered, who is involved in family work, when may it be offered, and how is family work offered and where.

In Section 2 we focus in detail on how to deliver family interventions in practice. In Chapter 7 (How to Prepare for Family Work Meetings) and Chapter 8 (How to Conduct Family Work Assessments) we concentrate on how to create an environment that is conducive to providing family work for psychosis. We propose that you will achieve this by first preparing yourselves as family workers and establishing your own support systems; only then should you go on to accept a referral and arrange to meet the service user and carers. We assert that the family work assessments you then carry out are also part of creating this conducive environment. In Chapter 9 (How to Manage a Successful Family Work Meeting) we describe how to bring the family together following the assessment process and how to actually deliver the recognised components of family work for psychosis. In addition, through these chapters we hope to help you manage the uncertainty that marks the start of the process, working with the family towards recovery.

We intend that each chapter can be viewed individually as well as provide an essential part of an integrated manual. For this reason when we mention another chapter we also give its full title the first time it is referred to in each chapter.

At the end of the manual we have included a glossary of terms. This allows us to maintain the flow of the text by avoiding the necessity to define some new at the point in each chapter where we use them for the first time. You will ...... be able to identify those words that are listed in the Glossary, as they appear in **bold** within the text.

Terms used within the manual

In this manual the terms 'service user' and 'carer' are used to refer to those who use mental health and social services, either directly or by association, as we feel it is necessary to adopt consistent terms to aid the flow of the text. We expect that some readers may experience difficulties with these terms and would hope that in practice workers will negotiate with individuals the terms that best suit them. We are aware that many people who are described by health and social services as carers would not necessarily label themselves as such, and may prefer to identify themselves by other terms, such as wife, father or landlady (Bainbridge 2002). To clarify our use of the word carer we have included a definition (written by a carer) as Appendix 2.

The term 'family work' is used to reflect the literature that has informed our practice and to differentiate the interventions described within this manual from systemic family therapy. All through the manual the term 'family worker' is used to refer to those who offer 'family work' or 'family interventions' (which are terms that we use interchangeably). We have chosen this term rather than 'therapist' or 'clinician' since staff may be working with carers in a range of settings, including residential homes and voluntary agencies or statutory services, and we feel it best describes our work in practice. As before, we hope that you will substitute this title with whatever term you feel most comfortable.

You will notice that we use the word 'illness' rather than 'disorder' or 'mental health problem'. We chose to stick with the word illness, in part because it demonstrates that family intervention embraces the medical model (Leff 1994), as well as social and psychological concepts. However, the stronger reason for this choice comes from carers themselves, who suggest that illness is the correct term as it embraces the magnitude of their situation better than disorder (Drage *et al.* 2004). Again, we expect workers to negotiate the right terminology with each family with whom they work.

Understanding the process of family work for psychosis

Often family workers are keen to get on with 'doing' family work; they rush into making the arrangements for when the work will take place and what difficulties will be addressed – the contract stage (see p.25). However, in order to fully engage families we feel there is necessary groundwork that needs to be covered first. Before beginning to develop new strategies through family meetings we advise that you first share the concept of family work to define what it is, to begin to understand the context in which it is offered and find out how best to **join** with (or contact) the family. In the long term we find that the time and energy invested in this preparation informs the contract and consequently improves our contact with carers and service users by clarifying our agreed purpose.

Concept

To conceptualise is to form an idea of something, which helps us to develop our understanding; in family work developing our own understanding and that of others is key to our interventions. In particular, it is important to develop an understanding of how each family is unique and avoid stereotypical pre-conceptions. This includes recognising what is understood by each family member and worker about the various ideas and theories related to psychosis embraced by psychiatry and within the family, and accepting that these will have different meanings to different people according to their individual knowledge and experiences. In relation to family intervention, the family will need to know and understand what family work is, so they have a clear idea of what is being offered and can make an informed choice about whether or not to engage.

One aim of this manual is to provide clarification about what family work is, as we feel this creates the foundation for good practice. Concepts about family work are explored and expanded throughout this manual, but covered mainly in this chapter and also in Chapter 2 (What is Family Work for Psychosis?).

When preparing to share the concept of family work, the following questions may offer a useful starting point for workers.

- What do I understand by family work and my role within it?
- How do my colleagues, managers and other local service providers understand family work?
- How will information about family work be shared with families?

Context

The context in which family work takes place is crucial, as it throws light on our purpose and meaning, while providing the family workers, the service user and carers with a boundary within which to operate. In this context we can also expressly acknowledge the stress that an illness such as psychosis can exert on a family system.

Within the context are the interrelated conditions in which the family and the workers find themselves, including family homes, workplaces, residential homes and hospitals, all shaped by individuals' experiences, beliefs, attitudes and culture. Bor and colleagues (2004) suggest that an appreciation of the social context will 'enhance a collaborative approach between therapist and client' (p.93); in our experience this is also true for the family worker, carer and service user.

In our model of family work we integrate aspects of the General Systems Theory (von Betalanffy 1968), which explores the family as a system within the systems that surround it; these systems may be useful in that they are supportive and promote coping or not (as described in Chapter 2). Nonetheless, in common with Kuipers, Leff and Lam (2002), we do not subscribe to the view held by some systemic therapists that the service user who experiences psychosis is 'the presentation by one family member of a "mad" family situation' (p.8).

The choice of assessments we use will inform our understanding of the context in which we meet each family. The assessment process and the purpose of the particular tools are mainly covered within Chapter 8 (How to Conduct Family Work Assessments). The impact of the context overlaps all sections in this manual and has a particular focus within Chapters 2, 3 (Why Offer Family Work for Psychosis?) and 6 (Where to do Family Work for Psychosis).

As behaviours, relationships and situations change so the context changes, which can make way for changes in understanding. So the context is fluid and in family work can change from meeting to meeting because meaning, purpose and intent can change.

Family members and workers may find it useful to ask themselves the following questions about context.

- Why are we considering family work now?
- What is the purpose of our meeting from perspectives of the family worker, mental health service providers, the service user and the carer?
- What brings us together?
- What are the issues that will affect our meeting together?

Contact

How we make contact within family work can make all the difference to how the process progresses (or doesn't, in some cases). Contact evolves through our communication and the relationships we form within the context of our overall aim of **joining** a family in their experiences of psychosis in order to offer help.

When in contact with each other all the family members and the workers will bring their personal experiences into the relationship; so an awareness of what we bring as workers in terms of our own beliefs, attitudes, skills, opinions and goals (both stated and not stated) is vital. We assert that this self-awareness cannot be found from reading books alone and that to achieve it we need to acknowledge and make use of feedback from our colleagues in practice, service users, carers, supervisors and trainers. Presenting family work as a learning opportunity for all concerned when explaining the concept will help to promote this awareness.

In this manual we are mindful throughout of the need for respectful contact with carers, service users and our professional colleagues. The focus on contact is provided in Chapter 4 (Who is Involved in Family Work for Psychosis?) and follows through with looking at supervision and co-working in Chapter 7.

Workers may find it useful to consider the following questions before making initial contact with a family.

- What transferable skills can I draw from other work that I do to use in family work?
- What do I bring that helps or hinders my relationship with others (family members, my co-worker or other professionals)?

Contract

A contract is an agreement made that defines what individuals will do together. Within family intervention a mutual understanding of the concept of family work, in the context of what is happening in each individual family and the contact that is possible, will help define what it is that we agree to do – namely the contract. Contracts are a fundamental aspect of family work and are explicit, usually in the form of a written agreement of what we will do and how we will be together in terms of respect for each other.

We have found that, before we get to problem solving or goal setting with families, preparation is extremely important. This may be likened to acknowledging that when an iceberg is viewed from the deck of a ship it is useful to remember that only the tip is observed and there is a large mass of ice hidden below the surface of the water. So it is with families: when we first meet them there is much that is not visible or overtly stated. Planning has the effect of making more of the picture visible or, as with the iceberg, it takes us below the surface of the water.

Sometimes, however, we will be asked to engage with problem solving before we have done any preparation because a family's immediate needs are so pressing (for example, when there is an imminent risk of relapse or carers are close to collapse). In such cases our flowchart comprising the whole process of family work (as shown in Figure 2.1) serves to remind us to complete the assessments with individuals at the earliest opportunity, to gather an awareness of everyone's perspective and strengths.

Collaborative agenda setting, requesting feedback, setting and reviewing homework, which are fundamental to effective family work, are likely to be discussed and agreed within the contract. These components are specifically explored and explained within Chapter 9 (How to Manage a Successful Family Meeting).

Workers and family members may find it useful to ask themselves the following questions when considering making a contract.

- What is it that we will agree to do?
- How will we manage any changes?

As these four elements (the concept, context, contact and contract) are developed through the family work process in a clear but flexible manner, then the understanding and trust between all concerned is likely to deepen. As they are developed, each informs another (as in a spiral), and can be revisited for further clarification, as shown in Figure 1.1, thus deepening our working relationships, and so on.

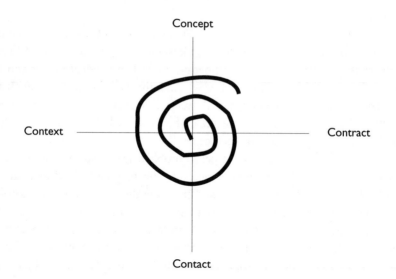

Figure 1.1 Interconnections between a concept, context, contact and contract

It is possible that as the family work progresses, some specific problems or needs that were not mentioned initially are shared; these may be difficulties such as dealing with criminal or abusive behaviour, past or present. Although the scope of this manual does not cover all these issues in detail, many of the principles we do deal with can help you and the families you work with to discuss and resolve such sensitive matters. We also give some pointers and suggest resources through which further support and/or information can be found.

An integrated approach

We propose that integration is key to all our work with families, linking the various components of the service user's (and possibly carer's) care plan with the family's strengths and resources. We are aware how much we use the word integration and its derivatives throughout the manual; we make no apology for this as we feel that no other word has quite the same meaning.

So what are we integrating? First, we aim to link theory and practice, bringing direction to practice from the evidence base. Our practice draws on work by Falloon, Boyd and McGill (1984), Barrowclough and Tarrier (1997) and Kuipers and colleagues (2002), as well as adopting a pragmatic stance based on our experiences in practice alongside that gained from training and supervising many others.

The experience of psychosis is not seen as being due to a single cause; it is seen as an illness that we understand to be very complex. Another of our aims is to integrate what we know about biological mechanisms, psychological processes and social influences to inform both our own understanding and that of the family. We see family members as being able to influence the course of the service user's illness, and do not believe it is useful or accurate to attribute the cause of the illness to carers.

Our approach is symptom led, rather than led by diagnosis, highlighting a willingness to work with diagnostic uncertainty and ambiguity (Birchwood, Fowler and Jackson 2000). Concentrating on the experience of mental illness and what this means for the carer and the service user provides a focus for the interventions described in this manual. In this way family work is **phenomenological**. Although most research concerning those who experience psychosis relates to schizophrenia, we also reflect on issues that are not diagnosis specific or that relate to other severe mental illness such as depression (Leff 2001) and bipolar disorder (Miklowitz and Goldstein 1997).

Through our intervention we aim to identify the needs of each family and each individual family member. The assessment process offers the opportunity to clarify these needs, as well as people's strengths. We can then select appropriate interventions, such as providing information, offering practical support or developing new skills within a context that promotes hope and recovery. Throughout our work we are mindful of joining the family, to build on strengths and bolster existing helpful coping strategies. We recognise that the ability to manage problems caused by illness can vary for each family member at different times. Our intention is to promote as much independence as possible for all those involved, at whatever pace is most appropriate and manageable.

Within this manual we do not attempt to review first-generation or subsequent family work studies in order to establish the effectiveness of family interventions in practice. This has been the subject of a number of systematic reviews (for example, Pharoah *et al.* 2005; Pitschel-Walz *et al.* 2001) and we feel its value is beyond doubt. Indeed, family work was expressly recommended in Britain in the National Service Framework for Mental Health (DH 1999) and is further endorsed in the National Institute for Clinical Excellence Guidelines for Schizophrenia (NICE 2002).

Nonetheless, some still dispute the effectiveness of family interventions (Dixon and Lehman 1995), finding that relapse is not really prevented, but merely delayed. However, we feel this is an unnecessary debate as it is known that each psychotic relapse increases the likelihood of a service user experiencing further psychotic relapses, as well as heightening the risk of residual symptoms remaining after the most acute psychotic symptoms have receded (WHO 1979). So it appears to us that even delaying a relapse (if that is really all that is possible) is in itself beneficial, as it reduces the total number of episodes of illness that a service user experiences in his or her lifetime. We also suggest that any delay is positive, by offering greater opportunities for both the service user and carers to develop interests and skills during the periods when the service user is well.

Summary

Family workers are advised to take Kipling's six honest men along with them when offering family interventions. While we remain mindful that over-analysis can sometimes make it difficult to decide what action to take, it is usually useful to ask the questions what, why, where, when, who and how before intervening in a new situation. However, when we are dealing with a crisis we sometimes just have to do the best we can with what we know at the time.

Prior to offering family interventions it is important for workers to have a good understanding of the concept, before deciding on the context and the contact and agreeing a contract. It is equally useful for service users and carers to have a fairly clear grasp of what family work entails before agreeing to participate, although there may be occasions when it is easier and/or more appropriate for workers to demonstrate the process in action by helping the family with an immediate concern rather than merely explain it in words.

Above all we urge you to remember that carers do not cause psychosis, but can do a great deal to influence its course. Family work provides a means to structure the help that mental health service providers offer to families and the help family members give to each other, so that effective strategies can be enhanced while the less useful ones are modified, replaced or discarded.

Key points

- Considering family interventions under the headings what, why, who, when, where and how can help workers grasp the overall process of family work in manageable 'chunks'.

- It is necessary for workers to fully understand the overall concept of family work before using it in practice.

- Family workers aim to understand the family's experience of psychosis before actively intervening.

- The knowledge and skills developed by experienced family workers are shared within this manual to help new workers develop their practice.

Recommended further reading

Bainbridge, M. (2002) 'Carers are People Too.' *Mental Health Today*, June, 24–27.

Birchwood, M., Fowler, D. and Jackson, C. (2000) *Early Intervention in Psychosis: A Guide to Concepts, Evidence and Interventions.* Chichester: Wiley & Sons.

Burbach, F. (1996) 'Family Based Interventions in Psychosis – An Overview and Comparison between Family Therapy and Family Management Approaches.' *Journal of Mental Health 5,* 2, 111–134.

Department of Health (DH) (1999) *National Service Framework for Mental Health.* London: The Stationery Office.

Leff, J. (1998) 'Needs of the Families of People with Schizophrenia.' *Advances in Psychiatric Treatment 4,* 277–284.

National Institute for Clinical Excellence (NICE) (2002) *Schizophrenia: Core Interventions in the Treatment and Management of Schizophrenia in Primary and Secondary Care.* London: NICE Guideline.

Recommended web-based resources

www.familywork.org.uk – Website for the Family Work for Psychosis Service provided by the Avon and Wiltshire Mental Health Partnership NHS Trust. It offers an overview of the family work process, information for professionals, service users and carers, and relevant literature and training courses. Links with other sites are listed.

www.gripinitiative.org.uk – GRIP offers advice and help to people in Gloucestershire experiencing their first episode of psychosis. This site introduces the service and offers information that is likely to be needed by service users and carers in a very helpful, accessible way. Links to other related sites are listed.

www.iris-initiative.org.uk – The Initiative to Reduce the Impact of Schizophrenia, known as IRIS, deals with early interventions for psychosis. It has a practical 'tool kit' for interventions and recommends guidelines on best practice for managing first-episode psychosis. It has suggestions for service development, how to conduct a care pathway audit, and research relating to reducing the impact of psychosis. It has information about training programmes and lists links to other related sites.

www.psychosissucks.ca —– Links to early intervention services in Canada. It offers useful information about psychosis in general and its management. There is information about treatment, recovery and other associated issues for service users and carers. It includes information and links to other relevant sites. It is particularly easy to use.

www.eppic.org.au – Links to early intervention services in Australia. It provides information about treatment for service users and carers, and includes links to other relevant sites.

www.thorn-cheltenham.org.uk – Provides information on an undergraduate degree-level course for workers, entitled Integrated Approaches to Managing Psychosis, also known as the Thorn Course, provided by the University of Gloucestershire. It includes links to national Thorn sites and a broad range of other related sites. It includes information about the research relating to managing psychosis and many other psychiatric illnesses.

www.hearingvoices.org.uk – Links to the Hearing Voices groups in Gloucestershire. Offers a summary of the group work, venues of groups in the locality, information and literature useful to service users, carers and professionals, including information about recovery. Lists links to other relevant sites.

www.rethink.org – Rethink is a non-statutory organisation that aims to help anyone affected by mental health problems. This site offers information to service users and carers about mental illness, treatments and recovery. It offers this information in a range of languages. It also offers guidance and support to those wishing to campaign for better services.

www.carershelpcarers.org.uk – Offers easy access to a mass of information for mental health carers, including the carers' information pack from which we have taken our definition of a carer, as shown in Appendix 2.

www.nmhct.nhs.uk/Pharmacy/ – This site is provided by the pharmacy service within Norfolk and Waveney Mental Health Partnership NHS Trust and supported on the Trust server. It receives no hidden commercial backing or bias, and was the first UK multi-page hospital pharmacy website. From here you can find out more about the drug treatments that are prescribed for mental health difficulties.

2

What is Family Work
for Psychosis?

What do we mean by family work for psychosis?

Family work for psychosis is an integrated approach (Gamble and Midence 1994). Its main purpose is to help a family within which one or more members are experiencing symptoms of psychosis to understand as much as possible about the illness and examine their intuitive coping responses and strategies. Through acknowledging that the symptoms of psychosis itself and the stress of coping with it can hinder communication (both in terms of giving and receiving information), families are encouraged to consider the value of using a structured approach to problem solving that has been found useful by many others in a similar situation (Falloon *et al.* 1984). This can help the family explore what is happening, to pool their resources and to reduce the potential for further disruption. Within this structured approach, where necessary, family members are helped to increase the effectiveness of their communication, by encouraging them to speak directly to one another and giving each other clear feedback about what they find helpful or unhelpful. This then allows adjustments to be made. The family worker's role is to make explicit and model desirable behaviours to facilitate the process. To best achieve this we recommend two family workers work with each family.

To discuss the elements of family work with others it is useful for us as mental health workers to have in mind a framework for the complete process, like the flowchart shown in Figure 2.1. As with any framework, it is not meant to be prescriptive but to help guide us and maintain our sense of purpose. We present our framework using a linear flowchart to display the process at its simplest, while recognising that sometimes it is necessary, for example, to go straight into problem solving or the education process in response to trying to manage an immediate crisis. Nevertheless, we urge you to remain mindful that when the groundwork has not been completed initially it will need to be visited at some point.

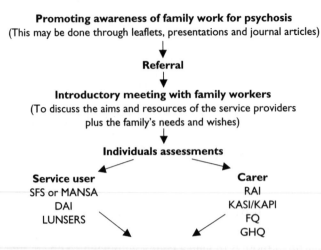

Promoting awareness of family work for psychosis
(This may be done through leaflets, presentations and journal articles)
↓
Referral
↓
Introductory meeting with family workers
(To discuss the aims and resources of the service providers
plus the family's needs and wishes)
↓
Individuals assessments

Service user	**Carer**
SFS or MANSA	RAI
DAI	KASI/KAPI
LUNSERS	FQ
	GHQ

First family work meeting
(Continuing the assessment process, encouraging family members to share what they have
discussed during their individual assessments, beginning to identify problems, strengths and needs)
↓
Education process
(This is a three-way process between the service user, carer and family
workers that builds on everyone's prior knowledge, beliefs and skills)
↓
Coping strategy enhancement and problem solving
↓
Evaluation and endings
↓
Booster sessions
(These allow any family member to ask workers to visit again once or twice a year after the
formal family work is complete, to allow them an opportunity to revisit any of the work done,
to strengthen the family's coping strategies or celebrate success)

Key to the assessments identified within the family work process flowchart

- **SFS:** Social Functioning Scale (Birchwood et al. 1990)

- **MANSA:** Manchester Short Assessment of Quality of Life (Priebe et al. 1999)

- **DAI:** Drug Attitude Inventory (Hogan, Awad and Eastwood 1983)

- **LUNSERS:** Liverpool University Neuroleptic Side Effect Rating Scale (Day et al. 1995)

- **RAI:** Relative Assessment Interview (Barrowclough and Tarrier 1997)

- **KASI:** Knowledge About Schizophrenia Interview (Barrowclough et al. 1987)

- **KAPI:** Knowledge About Psychosis Interview (local adaptation of KASI)

- **FQ:** Family Questionnaire (Barrowclough and Tarrier 1997)

- **GHQ:** General Health Questionnaire (28) (Goldberg and Williams 1988)

How to use these assessments and their purpose is described in detail in Chapter 8 (How to
Conduct Family Work Assessments).

Figure 2.1 Flowchart giving an overview of our integrated family work process

Carers and service users may also benefit from having an overview of the whole family work process to help them to better understand the purpose of what they are being offered. Appendix 3 offers an example of a simple handout that can provide this overview in an accessible conversational style. We find this handout also serves as a useful prompt for new workers when they are explaining the process to families.

Differentiating family work from family therapy

Within some systemic family therapy approaches an individual's symptoms of illness are seen as manifestations of a dysfunction within the **family system** (Corey 1996). A family work perspective is fundamentally different from this systemic approach in that the family is not seen as being in need of treatment. It is acknowledged that the environment where the service user lives (or systems to which he or she belongs) can have an effect on the course of the illness (Brown, Carstairs and Topping 1958; Brown *et al.* 1962). However, there is no suggestion (overt or otherwise) that families cause mental illness, there being no evidence for this (Hirsch and Leff 1975). Within family work any discussions about the cause of psychosis take place within a context of trying to understand sources of **vulnerability** and/or **stress**, in order to reduce the occurrence of future acute psychotic episodes.

Family work aims to capitalise on the carer's abilities and resources to help them to support the service user throughout the course of their illness, dealing with any problems caused by the illness (Barrowclough and Tarrier 1997). The focus of family work is generally on 'practical day to day issues' (Fadden 1998, p.164) in the here and now and not primarily on historical events. However, there will be times within the family work process when lessons may be learned from the past, particularly when planning relapse prevention strategies, so workers need to be able to explain, confidently and clearly, the difference between the cause and the course of psychosis. We recommend that new workers practise this skill through role play, either in the classroom or in supervision sessions, because (in our experience) a lack of clarity can lead to the risk of families feeling blamed and failing to engage with the family work process.

Components of family work

While there are recognisable components within any family work model – as listed in Box 2.1 and covered in detail in Chapter 9 (How to Manage a Successful Family Work Meeting) – we assert that the work itself should not be formulaic. Central to our work is respect for carers' feelings, experiences and strengths, as well as their problems and needs. A genuine working relationship between family workers and the family is important (Lam 1991), recognising that carers have a wealth of experience including coping strategies. In this we need to acknowledge the key role that carers often have in the decision-making process of, or for, the service user (Barrowclough and Tarrier 1997), especially in the early stages of recovery or when recovery is prolonged. The purpose of family work is to help share the enormity of the impact of psychosis, which is often described by families as catastrophic (Finkelman 2000), in an atmosphere that fosters hopefulness and reduces blame (Kuipers *et al.* 2002).

Box 2.1 Components embraced by most family interventions

Features that are present in all family work models include:

- promoting a collaborative working relationship
- using written documentation that is shared with the family
- an assessment process that elicits the family's strengths and ways of coping, which may offer opportunity for reminiscence and exploration of belief systems
- a forum for information exchange and education, which should be a three-way process (between the service user, carers and family workers) relating to significant events, diagnosis, medication, available mental health services and coping strategies
- optimal treatment for psychosis, including early signs monitoring, relapse prevention planning and the use of/or potential for using antipsychotic medication
- stress management by promoting clear communication to elicit problems, strengths and needs within the context of identifying and pooling resources to find solutions
- a problem-solving structure to provide a framework for working towards individuals' goals.

Ownership: whose problem is it?

Traditionally mental health services and society have tended to view the service user as an individual with a problem, and in many cases the service user came to be regarded as 'the problem'. Carers and the service providers would try to help the service user get over their problems, but often a lack of collaboration between the various parties concerned meant that each would have their own concept about the nature of the problem and would frequently find they were working against each other. Sometimes service providers came to view carers as part of the problem instead of viewing them as an ally; equally, at times, carers saw the mental health services (or lack of them) as exacerbating problems rather than resolving them. This created the potential for a culture of blame rather than cooperation, as well as leaving the service user in an isolated or powerless position, as depicted in Figure 2.2.

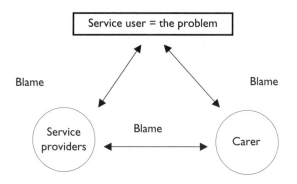

Figure 2.2 A non-integrated approach

The family work view differs by making it explicit that the illness is the problem, not the service user. All parties (the service user, carers and the service providers) are encouraged to see that they can have an influence on the illness and a part to play in the course that it will take. The family work approach is about pooling resources to create a greater coordinated force to combat the problems generated by the illness, as shown in Figure 2.3.

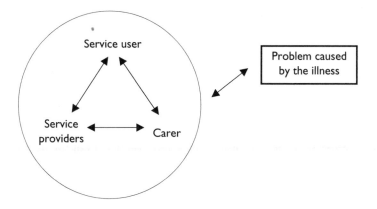

Figure 2.3 The family work approach

For this alliance to be achieved each party needs to be (and to feel) acknowledged and valued in order to own their part in the process, developing a sense of partnership through which the struggles caused by the illness may be navigated, as well as noticing strategies that work and celebrating successes.

In Box 2.2 we have provided a summary of what constitutes our integrated model of family work for psychosis.

Box 2.2 A summary of what we mean by family work

Our integrated model of family work:

- is a structured intervention that integrates biological, psychological and social models of psychosis
- aims for an alliance between the whole family and mental health service providers
- integrates what the family knows with the mental health workers' knowledge and skill
- provides a framework where the illness, not the service user, is seen as the problem
- is underpinned by stress vulnerability models, acknowledging that any severe illness can create high stress levels within any family
- builds on the family's strengths and ways of coping
- maximises clear communication within the family to help them manage problems most effectively
- is a 'no blame' approach in which individual's reactions are seen as a normal response to an abnormal situation.

It can be seen that family work builds on and develops alliances between service users, carers and all service providers (both statutory and voluntary) to work through problems caused by the psychosis, to try to find solutions that satisfy the needs of all concerned.

In family work we actively appreciate and listen to the expertise of every one involved:

- the *service user* for his or her first-hand experiences of the psychosis, and the skills that he or she uses to manage and cope with it
- the *carers* for their experience and observation of the psychosis, their knowledge of what it is like living in a family with someone who

has the illness and the skills they use to cope with it; some carers also help to further develop services that provide support and treatment to those who experience psychosis, as well as other carers

- the *mental health workers* for their knowledge, skills and experience gained through their professional training, and their collective experiences and knowledge gained from working with a number of service users and carers, which they apply in their intervention with each individual family.

We intend that the way we offer our thanks to each individual will demonstrate that we appreciate them for who they are rather than their actions and/or what they do for us. For example, in the phrase 'I really appreciate you for sharing that information with me' rather than 'I really appreciate that you shared that information with me' a difference in meaning is clear. In the former, recommended, statement it is the person sharing the information that is valued, in the latter it is the information itself that is valued.

Stress vulnerability models

Severe illness of any kind can create high levels of stress within families (Leff 1998). You may be able to relate to this if you have had personal experience of seeing how one relative's diagnosis, such as cancer, mental illness or heart disease, affected other members of your family. With psychosis this stress reaction is extremely common. Indeed it is suggested that the diagnosis of schizophrenia in a family member can, as we noted previously, be seen as a 'catastrophic event' by the whole family (Finkelman 2000, p.143).

Having some theoretical understanding of presenting problems (Clements and Turpin 1992) can help workers when **joining** with families. The frameworks that we find most useful are stress vulnerability models (for instance, Nuechterlein 1987; Zubin and Spring 1977), which suggest how an illness can develop due to possible contributing factors from an individual's vulnerability and environmental stressors, and how these may impact on each other. Simply, it can be said that the greater the vulnerability, the less stress is needed to precipitate the emergence of the **signs and symptoms** of illness. The interplay between stressors and vulnerability factors can cause a build-up of stress producing a state recognisable as a **prodrome**, which without intervention can become an acute episode of illness. It is also useful to note that some environmental factors (such as tolerant family relationships) may be protective and reduce the risk of psychosis emerging in a vulnerable individual.

Stress vulnerability models relating to psychosis embrace a number of different factors that leave an individual prone to developing an illness. Vulnerability may relate to the way information is processed (Duncan, Sheitman and Lieberman 1999), hyperactivity of the autonomic nervous system, personality traits (Nuechterlein and Subotnik 1998), neurotransmitter functioning such as dysregulation of dopamine (Harrison 1999), genetic sources (McGuffin, Farmer and Gottesman 1987), the intrauterine environment or early neural development (Torrey *et al.* 1994). Zubin and Spring (1977) also include external environmental aspects, such as birth complications and early life experiences or trauma, which can increase an individual's likelihood of becoming ill in later life. However, not all vulnerability factors leave the individual equally liable to develop a psychotic illness, nor do they exert the same effect on its course (Nuechterlein and Subotnik 1998), and vulnerability does not inevitably mean that an illness will occur. We find that carers and service users often appreciate being given this information by family workers and that it begins to create the culture in which everyone can share their individual views about the causes of psychosis (**causal attributions**) and begin to consider the way forward.

The stress vulnerability model described by Zubin and Spring (1977) is particularly valued by family workers due to its **face validity**. This model generally makes sense to service users and carers, while also having the flexibility to encompass the medical, psychological and social models used by the various service providers. It can bring the workers of a multi-disciplinary mental health team, voluntary services, the service user and carers together through a common understanding that does not necessarily include certainty about which diagnostic term is most appropriate, leading to clearer plans and interventions. It is our experience that, sometimes, care planning can be hampered by workers and/or carers focusing on the reliability and validity of a diagnosis (rather than offering help) while the service user continues to suffer. So a model that provides a way to understand the basis for intervention without a focus on diagnosis is extremely valuable.

As we listen to service users' and carers' experiences (Gregory 2001) we begin to understand the extremely stressful nature of living with psychosis, and that individual reactions (that can appear strange to the uninformed observer) may indeed be a normal response to an abnormal situation. The stress that carers and service users experience may be present within their living environment (and is known as ambient) or acute due to the additional pressures of coping with unexpected or particularly difficult life events. The higher the level of **ambient stress** the more likely it is that a stressful life event will precipitate an acute episode of psychosis in a vulnerable individual (Falloon and Shanahan 1990). Interventions may focus either on reducing ambient stress levels (by promoting clear communication, for example) or raising the threshold at which psychotic symptoms become unmanageable (for instance, through the regular use of

neuroleptic medication). Family work aims to embrace both possibilities, thereby offering the greatest likelihood that a psychotic relapse may be avoided.

We have found that not all families will relate to the graphical depictions of stress vulnerability models suggested by Zubin and Spring (1977) and Falloon and Shanahan (1990). Nevertheless, because the stress vulnerability concept is so central to understanding how family interventions work in practice it is worth workers persevering in trying to find a means to ensure each family's grasp of it. Some families will be helped to see and understand the interplay between vulnerability and stress through a concrete example. In such cases we have found it useful to offer the analogy described in Box 2.3.

Box 2.3 A wall used to depict a stress vulnerability model

A wall and its environment demonstrate the interaction between vulnerability and stress in the following way.

- The foundations of the wall equate to vulnerabilities; the stronger the foundations, the less vulnerable the overall structure will be.
- Stress equates to the number of bricks built up; the higher the wall the more likely it is to fall.
- Whether the wall falls depends on the interplay between its vulnerability and the stressors.
- Stress can be ongoing (or ambient), such as the weather, or acute, like a bulldozer.
- Cracks in the wall may be likened to early signs of psychosis.
- A wall is unlikely to fall down completely when it has been subject to stress.
- Strengthening the mortar equates to the use of mediating strategies, such as the use of medication or relapse prevention plans.
- If part of the wall does fall down it can be rebuilt. This will be achieved most easily with help and support from others.
- The wall may alter through the repair work; this does not necessarily make it better or worse than it was before.

A further means to explain the notion of a stress vulnerability model is offered in Box 2.4.

Box 2.4 An overflowing bath, depicting the relationship between vulnerability and stress

The image of a bath that may overflow shows the link between vulnerability and stress.

- Vulnerability relates to the bath's volume, or the size of the plug hole that allows water to escape.
- Stress equates to the amount of water flowing in to the bath.
- The threshold for psychosis can be thought of as the point when the bath overflows, because the amount of water coming in exceeds the amount escaping down the plug hole.
- Intervention may be seen in terms of reducing the flow of water into the bath or increasing the means for it to escape without flowing over the top of the bath.

Within stress vulnerability models, interventions can take many forms and be appropriate at various stages of preventing an illness or coping with its existence, thereby bringing optimism into practice. Family work is one such intervention in itself, embracing the medical, social and psychological aspects of functioning with an aim of reducing the stresses of living with psychosis. Family meetings can also become a forum for discussing the potential utility of other interventions, which may include:

- the use of medication
- relapse prevention planning
- individual cognitive behaviour therapy
- the use of complementary therapies.

It is worth noting that the service user's compliance with medication is often increased through family interventions (Falloon *et al.* 1984). This may well be because all members of the family will have had an opportunity to discuss the advantages and disadvantages of medication (including the long-term risks associated with taking it) within family meetings. This reduces the need for an individual who disagrees with the use of medication (whether this be the service user or carer) acting unilaterally to stop its use.

Family meetings also offer a place to discuss how the success of all interventions (including that of the family intervention itself) will be judged, within a context that appreciates that too-high expectations can be stressful. Such expectations can equally relate to the hope for a 'miracle cure' as much as to the pressure on a service user or carer to do more than is reasonably possible: to change an entrenched behaviour, for example, within too short a time frame. Thus family work provides a forum to establish realistic expectations, which may be understood within the framework of a stress vulnerability model, as summarized in Box 2.5.

Box 2.5 Summary of the value to family work of stress vulnerability models

Stress vulnerability models of psychosis:

- integrate biological, psychological and social factors
- view the nature of psychosis as episodic and related to stressful events
- acknowledge an individual's threshold above which acute psychotic symptoms emerge
- provide a framework to build on strengths and recognise the value of increasing an individual's capacity to deal with stress
- provide a rationale for identifying predisposing and precipitating factors, to monitor for early signs of psychosis and facilitate early interventions, highlighting the effect of ameliorating factors, such as medication and other coping strategies
- are not judgemental and attempt to understand the variables involved
- offer grounds for hopefulness and optimism
- view mental health and illness on a continuum.

Expressed emotion (EE)

During the early 1950s research began in London, monitoring the progress of patients leaving psychiatric hospitals (Brown et al. 1958). As predicted, those going to large, impersonal hostels relapsed quickly, but unexpectedly so did those returning to live with spouses or parents, while those living with siblings or landladies fared best. Further investigation (Brown et al. 1962) led to a realisation that the emotional climate within the service user's home was an influential factor effecting outcomes in schizophrenia.

Initially, Brown and colleagues used the term 'emotional involvement' to describe a carer's behaviour in relation to their relative, the service user. As their research progressed, however we can see them beginning to develop the concept of expressed emotion (EE) as a measurement of the emotional climate within the service user's home environment. There was an acknowledgement that reducing the amount of time the service user spent in contact with the carer within a highly emotional environment to below 35 hours per week reduced the service user's risk of relapse. There was however no suggestion from this research that family members were the cause of the illness, but rather that living with someone suffering from schizophrenia is stressful. This is well demonstrated by the following quotation: 'Once an illness has developed in one family member, a heightened level of tension is probably common. Once established, tense relationships in turn may have an important effect on the later stages of illness' (Brown *et al.* 1962, p.55). Indeed, it was recognised over a generation earlier 'that behaviour such as "over-protectiveness" may be the result of the patient's unusual behaviour influencing the parents' (Kasanin, Knight and Sage 1934, cited in Brown *et al.* 1962, p.55).

In the early 1970s Brown, Birley and Wing (1972) carried out a large study, replicating some of their previous work, in order to strengthen their findings; within this study the terms 'high' and 'low' EE were used. As expected, results revealed that service users returning to homes with high EE relapsed significantly more frequently over the nine-month follow-up period than those returning to a low EE environment. It was already recognised that service users with schizophrenia were sensitive to their surroundings due to an exaggerated physiological arousal (Venables and Wing 1962), and that either too much or too little stimulation could lead to reduced social functioning (Wing and Brown 1970); so it was that the 'optimum social environment was seen as a structured and neutrally stimulating one with little necessity for complex decision making' (Brown *et al.* 1972, p.241). Findings from this study formed the foundations upon which future family intervention studies were based.

Leff and colleagues (Leff *et al.* 1982; 1985) built on the knowledge gained from these previous studies, using a semi-structured interview schedule called the Camberwell Family Interview to measure the emotional environment of the service user's home. Over time they refined the measure into its current form which includes just three aspects on which to rate EE:

1.   critical comments

2.   hostility

3.   emotional over-involvement.

Their research supported the previous outcomes from Brown and colleagues (1962; 1972) and has since been corroborated by many later studies (reviewed by Bebbington and Kuipers 1994) demonstrating the association between relapse of schizophrenia and EE. This finding has been verified in a number of cultures and countries (Leff 1998).

The measurement of EE

The components that constitute EE have very specific meanings that allow any trained observer to rate them equally.

- Critical comments are rated on a frequency count. They are statements about resentment, disapproval or dislike of a service user's behaviour that are expressed with a critical intonation. For example, 'He is able to make himself a cup of tea, but he never offers me one.'
- Hostility is rated on a scale of 0–3. It is rated as present if a remark is made that indicates personal criticism of the service user (that is, comments made about the person themselves, not just their behaviour). For example, 'He has ruined our lives; he is evil.'
- Emotional over-involvement is rated on a scale of 0–5. This is extreme marked concern about the service user, with constant worry, overprotective attitudes and/or intrusive behaviour. For example, 'I can't let him out of my sight so how can I go out by myself?'

An overall rating of high EE is based on the presence of one or more of the following:

- six or more critical comments (seven in the early studies)
- marked emotional over-involvement (usually scored as high in the presence of three or more relevant comments)
- the presence of any hostility.

There is no scale for measuring low EE, so in the absence of high EE an environment is rated as low.

Translating the EE research into routine practice

Brown and colleagues (1972) had tried to clarify whether the service user's behaviour caused the carer's emotional reaction or whether it was the emotional environment that caused the illness. However, it proved difficult to 'specify the direction of cause and effect, but the fact that a decrease in expressed emotion at follow-up accompanies an improvement in the patient's behaviour strongly suggests there is a two-way relationship, each depending on the other' (p.255). Thus the studies of the influence of family life on the course of schizophrenia naturally led to the development of interventions that attempted to change EE from high to low, despite the remaining uncertainty about the cause and effect of the emotional interrelationship between a service user and their carer. Nonetheless, high EE is not a means of determining which families should receive intervention. This is highlighted in a study by Tarrier and colleagues (1988), which showed that some environments initially rated as low EE, where carers received only routine care during the course of the study, were rated as high at the end of the nine-month study period. Although this finding was not **statistically significant** it is important to us in practice as it highlights a risk to families if intervention is denied to them on the grounds that they are apparently coping well enough.

High EE is seen in environments in which professional carers work (Willetts and Leff 1997) as well as in family homes, and occurs in both mental and physical illnesses (Leff 1998). This suggests that the applicability of family work is far wider than the original research related to schizophrenia suggested, and that it could be hugely beneficial if many more workers across a whole range of service settings were trained and employed to work with families.

Workers must always remember that EE is a representation of a relationship and a measure of the emotional environment, not a personality trait of the carer (whether this is a family member, friend or professional worker). Specifically, it is intended as a means to rate 'the quality of the social interaction between carer and patient' (Scazufca and Kuipers 1996, p.580). Sadly this correct use of EE is sometimes lost and the consequent lack of understanding can lead to a label of high EE being employed pejoratively (Hatfield 1997). Even when the term is used appropriately, Johnstone (1993) noted, families may still feel blamed, so great care needs to be exercised if discussing the concept with carers. Indeed we would not recommend its use when explaining the purpose of family work to carers, but as so many carers now access research papers themselves and expect workers to discuss them it is vital that family workers have a good grasp of this research.

We have acknowledged that the measurement of EE was developed as a research tool and as such does not translate well for use in the clinical environment, due to the tendency of the interviewer to focus on measurement rather than developing a shared understanding of the situation. So how is the concept of EE useful in practice?

The knowledge gained in the studies about EE provides family workers with a framework for highlighting particular facets of communication and behaviour that can become the focus for interventions and directions for positive change. An example is a situation where a carer states critically about the service user that: 'She gets up when she needs to buy cigarettes for herself, but not when I ask her to go shopping for me.' This critical comment may represent a lack of understanding about the impact of psychosis on motivation, demonstrating a need for some education regarding the service user's **positive symptoms** and/or **negative symptoms**. It may also represent the carer's attempts to motivate the service user, which can usefully be **reframed** as an expression of concern rather than mere criticism. A further example would be a carer who buys her son's cigarettes because she fears for his safety when he goes out alone. This overprotective behaviour could again be reframed as a demonstration of caring, and in this case one that could be influenced by educating the carer that providing too much care may be counterproductive and actually increase the risk of psychotic relapse. Without the knowledge of the components of high EE the exact purpose of intervention would be less clear and could be interpreted by the carer as unfair criticism of their attempts to care.

Now we have the findings from previous research to guide our practice (summarised in Box 2.6), training in the measurement of EE is not necessary for working with families. Instead we can use the conversational style of family work assessments, as described in Chapter 8, to gain information that helps us to elicit the family's strengths, to turn problems into needs (and then into goals) in a way that avoids any hint of a blaming culture that could lead to seeing the user or carer as 'the problem'. In this way the process is needs-led rather than specifically about EE reduction. Nonetheless, we find that an understanding of some of the theory underpinning family interventions is likely to help workers feel more confident and creative by providing a conceptual framework that supports them.

Box 2.6 A summary of what we understand about high EE

High expressed emotion:

- describes an emotional environment characterised by significant amounts of criticism, hostility and/or emotional over-involvement expressed by a carer towards the service user
- is not a carer's personality trait
- has guided the development of family work, but does not translate well into practice; training to make this measurement is therefore not necessary for family workers
- and the service user's behaviour are interrelated
- is closely correlated with high levels of distress, influenced by carers' attributions.

As well as high EE, other factors were found to increase service users' relapse rates. These included recent decline in the ability to work, and lack of prescribed medication. The risk of relapse was highest for men below the age of 45 who had had a previous hospital admission (Brown *et al.* 1972). In practice, then, we need to ensure that a focus on EE does not blind us to other factors.

Attribution theories

As family workers trying to comprehend and make use of attribution theories in our practice, we have found the work of Barrowclough, Johnson and Tarrier (1994) to be particularly accessible and informative. This research offers a useful way to understand why the attitudes and responses of some carers to their relative (the service user with a diagnosis of schizophrenia) differ from the ways other carers respond. The study concludes that carers' beliefs about the cause of schizophrenia play a key part in their response to the service user, a finding that leads us as family workers to appreciate that exploring carers' causal attributions in relation to their relative's schizophrenia is crucial to our getting to know the family with whom we intend to work. Barrowclough and colleagues (1994) suggest that the attributions displayed by carers are a better predictor of the service user's likelihood of relapse than are the levels of EE.

While it is accepted that the reduction of EE within the home environment has provided a useful basis from which to offer family interventions, the concept is still rather poorly understood and, as previously discussed, conversations about EE are not usually helpful to relatives. Indeed the concept is likely to be perceived by carers as a criticism of themselves (Johnstone 1993). For us in practice, the measurement of EE does little to help explain why different carers respond differently to the service user's diagnosis, whereas discussing attributions about the possible causes of psychosis can be seen as an obvious means to begin a collaborative debate. Barrowclough and colleagues (1994) showed that exploring attributions is consistent with the descriptive accounts of EE from previous research, but without any implicit value judgements. To illuminate this further we will define what is meant by the term attribution and briefly explore the development of some attribution theories.

In his book *The Psychology of Interpersonal Relationships* (1958), Fritz Heider proposed that the actions people take will be based on their beliefs and that it does not matter whether those beliefs are valid or not. He stated that a psychologist needs to understand the belief (or causal attribution) held by an individual in order to understand his or her behaviour. Heider also explored the concept of internal and external attributions, showing how, for example, a person's belief about themselves (internal) and environmental factors (external) will help determine his or her behaviour. He found that people would filter out information that did not support their causal attributions in an effort to maintain simplicity, predictability and a sense of control.

Thus began the development of attribution theories. For example, Harold Kelley (1967) developed Heider's work by exploring what factors helped people form their attributions, which he described as the causes that a person ascribes to a situation, object or event, to make sense of their world. He identified and defined the following qualities that relate to attributions.

- Distinctiveness – the degree to which a person will behave differently in or with varying situations, objects or events.

- Consistency – the degree to which a person behaves in the same way towards a situation, object or event on different occasions.

- Consensus – the degree to which other people behave in the same way in or with the same situation, object or event.

Within the field of social psychology in the 1970s attribution theories proliferated, with many models being proposed and researched (for further explanation, see Hewstone and Stroebe 2001). One that we see as being particularly relevant to us in family work, as it is used in health and education services, is the psychosocial model known as the *Health Belief Model* (HBM) devised by Becker and Maiman (1975) which is discussed in more detail below (pp. 46–47).

Attribution theories look at the explanations people give to behaviours. They relate to the attribution (or reason) that an individual or group gives to the cause of situations or events. These attributions can then be explored to see how much they affect a person's thinking, which in turn may affect their responses and motivation.

There are basically two ways in which people attribute causes to events. Attributions may be external (or situational), which means that outside factors (including other people or objects) are given as an explanation. Alternatively, they may be internal (or dispositional), which entails an individual taking a personal responsibility for the factors that caused the event, and may relate to the individual's level of skill, knowledge or intelligence. Some people, particularly those in the western world, will readily give internal attributions to external situations. Examples of this include: 'He did not fill in the form because he was lazy' (when in fact the person being commented on may not have had a pen); or in the case of prejudice, 'They are all like that.'

Unfortunately, attributions are open to error. For example, Jones and Harris (1967) asked research participants to assess a writer's pro- or anti-Castro feelings by reading an essay. The participants were clearly told that the writer had been directed to write statements in support of or against Castro, and argue the case from that standpoint. Yet the participants were still convinced that the writer believed the content of the writing, despite having been given information that the writer was following instructions. This is an example of what is known as a fundamental attribution error.

Western society tends to have a strong blame culture in which people generally look for one attribution or a single reason for something happening, when in reality there is usually more than one attribution for any given situation. It is worth noting that 'people tend to give external attributions to things that happen to them and internal ones to things that happen to others' (Jones and Nisbett, cited in Barrowclough *et al.* 1994, p.85).

Attributions such as prejudices can be held by an individual, a group or part groups of people, so there can be a number of permutations within any group with partial external and/or internal attributes. Look again at the section regarding the ownership of the problems caused by an illness discussed earlier in this chapter and you will see numerous variations of how service users, carers and mental health service providers could attribute each other's behaviours, externally or internally. You can probably also relate these to the terms 'distinctiveness', 'consistency' and 'consensus' as defined by Kelley (1967).

Attributions have a part to play in terms of how members of a family may respond to their relative's illness. For example, Brown and colleagues (1972) found that families who were more tolerant of unusual behaviour created an atmosphere that helped maintain the service user's well-being. Tolerance is thought to be informed by the attributions carers hold regarding the service user's unusual behaviour, with more relaxed attitudes accompanying external attributions (Barrowclough, Tarrier and Johnson 1996), which means believing that the service user cannot control his or her behaviour. There is a risk, however, that such attributions can lead to emotional over-involvement if these beliefs extend to seeing the service user as very fragile. Conversely, internal attributions through which the service user is perceived as being able to take control can induce critical comments as the carer displays his or her frustration and/or attempts to prompt recovery.

As well as looking for causes of the illness that relate directly to the service user's behaviour, carers are likely to have attributions about their own part in its development. This is particularly relevant to us within family interventions if carers are expressing beliefs that suggest they are blaming themselves for the occurrence of psychosis (demonstrating internal attributions), and are suffering guilt and distress accordingly (Barrowclough *et al.* 1996).

To further understand carers' and service users' responses to illness it can be useful to employ an HBM, in order to explain and predict health-related behaviours, which may be explored by focusing on the attributions ascribed by individuals to a given healthy/unhealthy situation. Our purpose as family workers is well served by the HBM described by Becker and Maiman (1975), which comprises four main beliefs that contribute to maintaining well-being that can be explored through the family work process.

1. Perceived susceptibility or vulnerability; for example, propensity to illness or relapse.

2. Perceived severity; for example, a belief that a relapse would not have a negative outcome.

3. Perceived benefits; for example, a reduced susceptibility or being symptom free.

4. Barriers to adherence or negative aspects of recommended behaviour; for example, stigma, side effects, the effort required to comply with treatment or the financial cost.

The utility of this HBM within family interventions is supported by research conducted by Adams and Scott (2000) in a small study of 39 service users with psychosis, looking at their adherence to medication. The findings showed that this HBM could be useful in helping identify the service users that may find it difficult to adhere to medication. Service users fully agreeing to take medication had significantly different perceptions of their illness, self-beliefs and the control they had over the illness from those who were non-compliant. For those that did not take their medication regularly, the perceived severity of illness and perceived benefits of treatment accounted for 43 per cent of the differences in adherence behaviour.

Attributions and family work for psychosis

Clearly, then, it is likely to be useful if we have some idea of the beliefs that carers, service users and our mental health worker colleagues hold, in order to help us join with the family members in their endeavour towards positive and healthy outcomes. Family workers also need to quite clearly understand their own causal attributions relating to the problems experienced by the service user, and ask themselves how this fits, or doesn't fit, with the carer's and service user's attributions. Importantly, this allows us as family workers to balance our perceptions and preconceptions with the information we gain from carers, service users and other service providers about the attributions they hold at any given point. Attributions are seen as responses to seeking explanations and a 'greater causal search [more attributions] will indicate higher levels of distress' (Barrowclough *et al.* 1996, p.692). This helps us understand that the high EE that is sometimes observed in a family environment is likely to be a manifestation of distress.

Attributions, as summarised in Box 2.7, as well as EE have been found to change through family interventions (Brewin 1994), demonstrating that they are not stable traits: they generally change as information and experiences are processed by individuals.

Box 2.7 A summary of why it is useful for family workers to consider attributions

Attributions:

- can be viewed as a response to asking the question 'Why?'
- need to be central to the discussions through which family workers begin to engage carers to form a collaborative working alliance
- are better explored through discussing experience and reflection than through didactically teaching and giving information
- theories can help family workers understand the differing attitudes and responses to caring demonstrated by carers.

Summary

Family work is an integrated psychosocial approach to working with service users and carers. By joining the 'family' in a collaborative manner, family workers build on the strengths within the family system integrating biological, psychological and social models (what we know) with the carers' and service users experiences and responses (what the carers/service users know).

The primary purpose of family work is to use a structured process to work through problems, clarify communication and help families coping with psychosis or other serious mental health problems.

Family work uses stress vulnerability models to provide a theoretical framework through which people can understand how psychosis develops. It is underpinned by the theory of expressed emotion, although carers' attributions are a better predictor of psychotic relapse than expressed emotion. Our family work model is a co-working model, which means two family workers work with each family.

Key points

- The primary purpose of family work is to help families coping with psychosis to understand as much as possible about the illness, in order to recognise their intuitive ways of coping and develop new strategies as necessary.

- Family work helps family members communicate clearly and use a structured process to work through problems to deal most effectively with the service user's psychosis.

- Family work uses stress vulnerability models to provide a theoretical framework through which people can understand how psychosis develops and how relapses can be averted or minimised.

- Family work is underpinned by the theory of expressed emotion (EE), which provides a rationale for some suggested behavioural changes.

- Our family work model is a co-working model, which means two workers work with each family so that they can model, as well as make explicit, ways to communicate effectively.

- Individuals' responses to illness and willingness to accept treatment can be explained through the Health Belief Model (HBM) devised by Becker and Maimon (1975).

- Carers' attributions are a better predictor of psychotic relapse than is expressed emotion.

Recommended further reading

Barrowclough, C., Johnson, M. and Tarrier, N. (1994) 'Attributions, Expressed Emotion and Patient Relapse: An Attributional Model of Relatives' Response to Schizophrenic Illness.' *Behaviour Therapy 25*, 67–88.

Barrowclough, C., Tarrier, N. and Johnson, M. (1996) 'Distress, Expressed Emotion and Attributions in Relatives of Schizophrenia Patients.' *Schizophrenia Bulletin 22*, 4, 691–702.

Barrowclough, C. and Tarrier, N. (1997) *Families of Schizophrenic Patients* (2nd edn). Cheltenham: Stanley Thornes.

Clements, K. and Turpin, G. (1992) 'Vulnerability Models and Schizophrenia: The Assessment and Prediction of Relapse.' In M. Birchwood and N. Tarrier (eds) *Innovations in the Psychological Management of Schizophrenia*. Chichester: Wiley & Sons.

Drage, M., Floyd. S., Smith, G. and Cocks, N. (2004) *Evaluating Family Interventions: A Qualitative Investigation*. Bath: University of Bath. Available at www.familywork.org.uk.

Falloon, I. and Shanahan, W. (1990) 'Community Management of Schizophrenia.' *British Journal of Hospital Medicine 443*, 62–66.

Gamble, C. (2000) 'Using a Low Expressed Emotion Approach to Develop Positive Therapeutic Alliances.' In C. Gamble and G. Brennan (eds) *Working with Serious Mental Illness. Manual for Clinical Practice.* Edinburgh: Bailliere Tindall.

Hatfield, A. (1997) 'Working Collaboratively with Families.' *Social Work in Mental Health: Trends and Issues 25,* 3, 77–85.

Hewstone, M. and Stroebe, W. (eds) (2001) *Introduction to Social Psychology.* Oxford: Blackwell.

Kuipers, E., Leff, J. and Lam, D. (2002) *Family Work for Schizophrenia* (2nd edn). London: Gaskell.

3

Why Offer Family Work
for Psychosis?

Why offer family work for psychosis?

The question 'Why offer family work for psychosis?' can be framed in all sorts of ways from many different sources and from a range of perspectives. As family workers you may be asked questions such as the following.

- 'Why is it so important to include family work as an integral part of mental health services?' (General)

- 'Why should we use our hard-pressed resources on a process that seems to be so time consuming and labour intensive?' (Managers)

- 'What will we have to cut back on to be able to allow time for family work?' (Workers)

- 'It is our relative who is ill, so why do *we* need to see you?' (Carers)

- 'Why would you want to see my family?' (Service user)

We see these as genuine questions born out of viewing mental illness as being the problem solely of the service user, as discussed in Chapter 2 (What is Family Work for Psychosis?). Traditionally mental health services have been geared towards individual treatment and responses. Yet the shift from hospital-based services to community care demands that mental health workers align themselves with the carers (DH 1999; Grad and Sainsbury 1963; NICE 2002), accepting that statutory service providers are now largely dependent on **informal carers** for the majority of care giving. Family work provides a structure whereby mental health workers and carers can find working together more satisfying and effective.

Burden

Family burden is generally defined in terms of the negative impact on carers that comes from living with a mentally ill person (Webb *et al.* 1998). It may be subjective, which means that it is felt, or objective, such as resulting in actual financial hardship (Hoenig and Hamilton 1966), and can, in either manifestation, rmful effect on the carer's physical, social and/or psychological (Fadden, Bebbington and Kuipers 1987).

ıne stresses of caring for a family member who has a long-term illness can be high, often leading to further stresses, including anxiety or depression (for both the service user and carers) as carers tend to become overwhelmed and exhausted. It appears that burden for one family member is frequently associated with poor performance from another (Platt 1985). This is particularly closely related to social performance, and its existence 'indicates the breakdown of the reciprocal arrangements that people maintain in their relations, such that one person is doing more than their fair share' (Fadden *et al.* 1987, p.285).

Care-giving responsibilities frequently lead to social isolation. This isolation and burden may relate to the guilt (Drage *et al.* 2004) and the experience of stigma that carers frequently report in relation to the service user's diagnosis of psychosis (Ostman and Kjellin 2002).

Stigma

Goffman (1968) defined stigma as a term used to describe 'an attribute that is deeply discrediting' (p.13), which leads to discrimination due to a belief that 'the person with a stigma is not quite human' (p.15). As such the term may relate to race or religion, a physical disfigurement or moral weakness (the category into which Goffman places mental illness).

Stigma is an important consideration for us as family workers as it has been shown to contribute to disruption within a family due to its negative effects on the self-esteem of the service user (Wahl and Harman 1989). Unfortunately, it appears that stigma may be increased when the general public hold an illness model as opposed to viewing the condition as a response to overwhelming environmental stressors (Mehta and Farina 1997). This medicalised view is reinforced repeatedly by media headlines that include the diagnosis of schizophrenia (correctly and incorrectly) when reporting tragic or violent acts related to an individual suffering from any mental illness.

A review by Read (2002) found that people who embrace the medical model are more likely to reject the schizophrenia sufferer, who then has less likelihood of forming friendships. This view is informed by psychoanalytic theory (Read 2002), which finds that people's fear of succumbing to psychosis leads to increased stigmatisation and consequently their harsher treatment and/or rejection of service users. This fear is compounded by a belief that people with mental health problems are not responsible for their actions, which the public associates with the risk of unpredictable behaviour and violence. This creates a vicious circle whereby service users are shunned and consequently have no visible opportunity to demonstrate that the general public perception of mental illness is inaccurate.

However, it is known that stigma can be countered when we get to know the person with a diagnosis of mental illness as an individual, by hearing their personal story (Penn *et al.* 1994). Family work can therefore play a significant role in reducing stigma by encouraging people (both service users and carers) to share their experiences of psychosis to inform and educate others. This may be facilitated by the family work assessments and education process that can help carers and service users develop their own understanding, which some may go on to use to promote a greater awareness in others.

Grief and guilt

It is usual within family work to keep the service user central to the process, which means the focus tends to be on assisting carers to help the service user. Unfortunately this can sometimes lead to mental health service providers neglecting the needs of the carers themselves. Carers can perpetuate this situation, especially in the earliest stages of coping with psychosis (Mohr, Lafuze and Mohr 2000), either by failing to acknowledge their own needs or willingly being self-sacrificing in order to focus all available resources on the service user.

However, we believe that at times a carer's needs are paramount, particularly when his or her feelings of grief and bereavement are predominant. It has been found that relatives who respond to the service user's psychosis with high levels of grief tend to deny rather than accommodate the experience (Patterson, Birchwood and Cochrane 2000), with an ongoing likelihood that they remain remote. Therefore, specific grief therapy such as the use of reminiscence (Miller *et al.* 1990; Miller 1996) may be helpful (or even vital) before carers in this emotional position try to take on a rehabilitative role with the service user. By encouraging carers to acknowledge and thereby accommodate their losses, as discussed in Chapter 9 (How to Manage a Successful Family Work Meeting), coming to accept different expectations for both their own lives and that of the service user, we would hope to prevent denial, which has been found to lead to entrenched patterns of critical attitudes (Patterson *et al.* 2000). Without appropriate intervention, the strong sense of responsibility felt by carers that can come from suppressed feelings of guilt, shame and sometimes self-blame, often referred to as 'the burden of care', is likely to increase over time (Fadden *et al.* 1987, p.285).

It is important to remember that grief is not in itself a pathological response that needs treatment – it is in fact a normal, healthy response that all human beings experience at times of loss to help them adapt to a new situation. So grief is not an illness and does not generally need treatment with medication, but what the grieving person does tend to need is an acknowledgement of what they are going through. For example, a father had difficulty in acknowledging his grief that his son was not able to follow him as planned into the family business due to the son's experience of psychosis. With help and encouragement he was able to grieve; he could then move on, begin to accept their situation and plan for a different future for them both.

At this stage we feel it is useful to examine some dictionary definitions of grief to begin to explore how it can affect those involved in caring for someone experiencing psychosis. These, drawn from *The Concise Oxford Dictionary* (1998) include the following meanings:

- the act or instance of losing, which may include a person, thing or an amount of something that is lost
- the detriment or disadvantage that results from losing something
- the state of being lost: at a loss, feeling puzzled, not knowing what to do
- a deep or violent sorrow; a keen regret.

Colin Murray Parkes (1998) offers us an explanation of grief as an emotion that comes out of an awareness of the difference between what is and what should be. This appears to fit with the feelings described by many carers, as well as service users and some mental health workers, in the context of psychosis.

Parkes (1998) also explores the phenomenon of **psychological transitions**, which all human beings meet at certain stages in their lives. We experience many such psychological transitions throughout our lifetime, including birth to infancy, childhood to adolescence, adolescence to adulthood, and so on, as we let go of one part of life to move on to another. Within this framework, grief is seen as a natural part of the transition, through the process of expressing loss, and usually it is not overtly expressed unless a keenly felt regret interferes with an individual's functioning. As the word transition suggests, grief is not a permanent state, but anyone can become stuck at any point, particularly if there are complications or an ongoing state of confusion. It is easy to see, therefore, how carers and/or service users may become stuck in their process of grieving due to the fluctuating and unpredictable nature of psychosis.

Resilience and coping

The concept of resilience is well described by Marsh and colleagues (1996) as 'the ability to rebound from adversity and prevail over the circumstances of our lives…based in part on personal disposition, on the nature of the family, and on the community of people who provide support' (p.4). We feel that this concept provides a balance for that of family burden (Lefley 1996), which is useful to us as family workers in providing a theoretical framework to promote our understanding of why some carers appear to cope more successfully than others. Indeed, it appears that the recognition of the positive aspects of their role forms part of a carer's coping response. Therefore it is proposed (Marsh *et al.* 1996) that mental health service providers should design services for families in a way that not only reduces family burden, but also maximises and capitalises on a family's resilience. All mental health workers can achieve this (Lefley and Johnson 1990) by working collaboratively with families to promote a mutual respect and acknowledgement of all parties' contributions. Unfortunately this is not always the case in current mental health practice, so it is likely that family workers will in some cases need to play an advocacy role to facilitate the development of these collaborative relationships.

There are many theories relating to coping and family stress (Lefley 1996) and to explore them all is way beyond the scope of this manual. Instead we have tried to capture their essence, defining coping as 'the things that people do to avoid being harmed by life's strains' (Pearlin and Schooler 1978, p.2).

Mohr and colleagues (2000), describing the National Alliance for the Mentally Ill (NAMI) approach to supporting families, placed coping within a process of accommodating trauma. The first phase, denial, was not seen as maladaptive but a means 'to avoid the painful reality of the personal disaster with which the family has been confronted [and the] needs of the family at this time are comfort, support, empathy and assistance in finding resources' (p.238). This probably represents the point when professionals could most usefully engage with families (Kuipers *et al.* 2002) to facilitate the second stage, learning to cope. Family members have been seen to demonstrate and express feelings of guilt, anger and grief at this time, probably in response to the uncertainty of their situation. Mohr and colleagues (2000) found that collaboration with service providers, including some skills training and contact with other carers, was most helpful. It appears that coping is linked to 'letting go' (p.238). The third stage is marked by understanding, acceptance and an active advocacy role, which is thought to counteract feelings of loss.

Family work for psychosis could be summarised as a psychosocial approach designed to maximise the ways service users and carers cope with psychosis. This coping is influenced by the individual's own resources and personal qualities such as resilience as well as the support received from those around him or her (including those from mental health service providers); stigma exerts a negative influence.

Promoting collaboration between mental health service providers and carers

There is a strong correlation between the stress of caring for someone with a long-term illness and high EE (Scazufca and Kuipers 1996), in physical as well as mental illnesses (Leff 1998). Knowing this allows us to reappraise critical comments or high levels of emotional involvement as outward signs of stress and an expression of distress, as discussed in Chapter 2. Helping carers understand the symptoms of psychosis can help them reattribute to illness behaviour that they may previously have misattributed to a personal character trait of the service user (Barrowclough *et al.* 1994). This in turn can help reduce critical comments and/or emotional over-involvement and engage the carer in different ways of behaving, thus reducing the background stress and tension for all concerned.

We also know that people who experience mental illness do a lot better in life if they have the support of their families (Hatfield 1997). This paradigm shift, with its change in focus from viewing families as **pathogenic** and dysfunctional to seeing them as basically competent, is further informed by the increasing evidence for biological explanations for schizophrenia (Andreason 1984), as well as a lack of evidence (Hirsch and Leff 1975) to support the theories that left families feeling blamed for causing schizophrenia. This aligns us with a perspective that places an emphasis on wellness, strengths and resources rather than illness, weakness and liabilities, allowing carers to become allies instead of being excluded from service provision, and consequently to begin to gain control over their own lives (Mohr *et al.* 2000). As family workers it is important for us to keep this perspective central to our process, to ensure we build on the ways that family members lived well together, prior to the onset of psychosis, and not make assumptions about the causes of psychosis.

It is worth noting that of all the available psychosocial interventions, family work has most consistently been shown to be effective (DH 1999), with positive outcomes including the reduction in levels of carers' burden and reducing relapse rates for service users suffering from schizophrenia. There are further benefits to be gained by working with carers that arise from the partnership derived from family interventions. It has long been asserted that to have knowledge equates to having power; carers often complain that they are denied information, which leaves them feeling powerless (Smith 2003). Leff and colleagues (2001) found that collaboratively sharing knowledge between the service user, carer and mental health workers helped empower them all in their decision-making processes, especially with regard to the use of medication. Family work can also help carers to support the service user in a way that leads to better social functioning (Falloon *et al.* 1984; McFarlane 2000) and an improved quality of life (Zastowny *et al.* 1992).

As mental health workers we have seen both for ourselves and in the practice of some of our students and supervisees that providing family interventions can be beneficial to family workers themselves. Often carers have a wealth of experience that can help us, both in our work with particular families and more broadly in our own personal and professional development (DH 2004). Frequently the family work reduces the need for carers to randomly contact service providers when they are in distress or, even worse, feel they have to complain to get support.

This means that workers' contact with carers can be constructive rather than defensive, which in our experience is a much more satisfying way of working, sometimes even encouraging carers to join the mental health workforce themselves.

Government policy supporting family work for psychosis, and its economic benefits

There is an economic rationale for providing family interventions (Leff *et al.* 2001). The number of studies that have included a financial breakdown is limited (Lam 1991), but where an analysis has been carried out (Falloon *et al.* 1984; Tarrier *et al.* 1988), family work has been shown to be cost effective. These evaluations take account of both the reduction in the number of days service users spend in hospital, due to lower relapse rates (Tarrier *et al.* 1994), and the cost of the family work itself, which includes the costs of providing the training required by practitioners to enable them to deliver these effective family interventions (Leff *et al.* 2001).

In Britain family intervention is also congruent with government policy and legislation regarding mental health care services. Through the White Paper *The New NHS: Modern Dependable* (DH 1997), there is a shift in the emphasis from one where the service provider's effectiveness was measured in purely economic terms, to a position in which the quality of the service delivered is also monitored for its effectiveness in practice through **clinical governance**. The National Service Framework for Mental Health (DH 1999) provides information on the effectiveness of many interventions and within this document family work is endorsed at the highest level. More recently, the British government has published a number of guidelines through the National Institute for Clinical Excellence (NICE) to steer services further towards best practice. One such guideline relates specifically to schizophrenia (NICE 2002), yet again stating the importance of offering family interventions at every available opportunity. The evidence in support of family interventions is so compelling that workers in other countries may well find that their own government has produced similar legislation to promote family work in practice.

Family work for psychosis obviously has a part to play in championing collaborative working practices. However, the word carer is not limited to caring for a service user experiencing psychosis and indeed is more often associated with services working with older people. So the endeavour to establish carers' assessments as stated in Standard 6 of the National Service Framework for Mental Health (DH 1999) will need to go beyond providing family work for psychosis within everyday practice. Nonetheless, linking the total requirement of this standard to family interventions' strong evidence base can help promote carers' assessments generally within a clinical governance framework. This may then increase the likelihood they will be offered to those caring for service users across a wide range of mental illnesses, with the possibility that family interventions may also develop beyond helping families coping with psychosis.

Summary

Box 3.1 provides a summary of the reasons why family work should be available to all families coping with psychosis. We hope this will provide you with all the answers you need when questioned, as you try to implement it within your practice area.

Box 3.1 Reasons why family work should be available within routine practice

Family work should be offered because it:

- effectively combines the resources of the carer and service user with those of mental health service providers
- offers a framework for collaborative decision making, with an emphasis on promoting informed choices
- is known that family support can improve outcomes for service users, including a reduction in the number of acute episodes of illness that they are likely to experience
- improves collaboration and choices made about medication, thereby increasing the service user's adherence to his or her treatment regimen
- minimises the damaging experience of struggling alone that so many carers have endured
- has a broad impact on the caring role, including its social, emotional, psychological and physical aspects
- gives access to information, emphasising a three-way process between service users, carers and service providers, with an opportunity to redress any imbalances of power
- has benefits for mental health workers
- is evidence based and is recommended within many government policies
- can begin the process of breaking down the stigma associated with living with psychosis.

Key points

- Research has repeatedly shown that family interventions reduce psychotic relapse rates.

- Family work for psychosis promotes a positive working relationship between mental health service providers, service users and carers that improves outcomes for all concerned.

- Many government policies and good practice guidelines support the provision of family interventions.

- High expressed emotion (EE) is not a carer's character trait, but a manifestation of distress. Family work for psychosis offers a means to explore this distress and change the behaviours that create a high-EE environment.

- Family interventions promote proactive rather than defensive mental health practice.

- Being able to communicate clearly and use a shared structured process helps family members work through problems to achieve their goals.

- Family interventions are cost effective.

Recommended further reading

Brooker, C. and Repper, J. (eds) (1998) *Serious Mental Health Problems in the Community.* Edinburgh: Bailliere Tindall.

Lam, D. (1991) 'Psychosocial Family Interventions in Schizophrenia: A Review of Empirical Studies.' *Psychological Medicine 21*, 423–441.

Mohr, W., Lafuze, J. and Mohr, B. (2000) 'Opening Caregiver Minds: National Alliance for the Mentally Ill's Provider Education Program.' *Archives of Psychiatric Nursing 14*, 5, 235–243.

Ostman, M. and Kjellin, L. (2002) 'Stigma by Association.' *British Journal of Psychiatry 181*, 494–498.

Pharoah, F., Rathbone, J., Mari, J. and Streiner, D. (2005) 'Family Intervention for Schizophrenia (Review).' The Cochrane Library, Issue 4. West Sussex: Wiley Press.

Pitschel-Walz, G., Leucht, S., Bauml, J., Kissling, W. and Engel, R. (2001) 'The Effect of Family Interventions on Relapse and Rehospitalisation in Schizophrenia: A Meta-Analysis.' *Schizophrenia Bulletin 27*, 1, 73–92.

Wykes, T., Tarrier, N. and Lewis, S. (1998) *Outcome and Innovation in the Psychological Treatment of Schizophrenia.* Chichester: Wiley & Sons.

4

Who is Involved in Family Work for Psychosis?

Creating a climate conducive to family work

Traditionally many mental health services concentrated on individual work with service users. This focus is now changing, with a growing recognition of the effectiveness of family interventions and demands for the needs of carers to be incorporated into mental health service delivery (DH 1999), thus creating an environment in which it is becoming increasingly possible to integrate family work into routine practice.

When a family begins to perceive a problem (whether or not it is recognised as psychosis), the first place they are likely to turn to for help is their general practitioner (GP) or another member of the primary care team (PCT). It is therefore essential that PCTs are aware of family interventions and are able to make a referral to relevant services if they feel it is needed. In some cases the need for a formal referral may be unclear and an informal discussion is more appropriate; strong links between primary and secondary mental health care services facilitate these discussions and can help prevent unnecessary delays in families gaining the support they need (Smith 1999). In some areas a direct referral for family work from primary care is not possible and is available only once the service user is in receipt of secondary care because of the way services are organised. In such cases the GP or other PCT member can ensure (probably through leaflets provided by family workers like the one shown in Appendix 4) that carers are aware of family work, so that they can ask the mental health service providers for it at the earliest opportunity.

Voluntary organisations such as the Citizen's Advice Bureau may be another place that families dealing with the impact of unrecognised psychosis go to seek help. Therefore, these also need to be aware of the family work resources that are available in their locality and how families may access them. This would apply equally to counsellors, including those working in private practice.

In some cases where carers have found out about family work themselves from a source outside of their local mental health service provision (such as a national mental health charity, friends or other carers) they may try to access services directly. An open, welcoming, referral system can facilitate this approach by carers if working with carers is accepted as part of a comprehensive mental health service provision (Smith 1999). Nevertheless, the Care Programme Approach (DH 1990a, 1990b) remains an important means of coordinating the service user's care, and it is recommended that, no matter the route by which families access family work, it is eventually included in a written care plan. It has been found that when family work is not incorporated in this way, the interventions appear less effective (McFarlane *et al.* 1995).

As highlighted above, collaboration is an important part of the service provision. Specialist mental health services need to evolve a collaborative approach, not only between themselves, other organisations and families, but also within their own systems. A multi-disciplinary approach that integrates health and social services' resources (DH 1995) can facilitate this. Family work within this model is not perceived as a specialist service or an add-on, but an integral part of the overall service provision. Therefore, skills in working with families need to be developed within teams as part of their core competencies. Ideally, working in partnership with carers should be an explicit part of every mental health team's operational policy and included in any promotional literature about the local service provision.

Competence in practice

A great number of mental health workers have long been aware of the positive influences of family members on the course of schizophrenia. For example, many community psychiatric nurses pragmatically worked with families, particularly in rural areas, but this was often on an ad hoc basis and according to the interest or dedication of the nurse involved, rather than as part of a service that was formalised through the community mental health team's (CMHT) operational policy. However, some workers misconstrued the families' experiences and in such cases carers were seen as causing the illness (Bateson *et al.* 1956; Laing and Esterson 1964). Sadly, despite a lack of evidence to support these accusations (Hirsch and Leff 1975), a blaming attitude contaminated the minds of many mental health professionals (who possibly did not understand the concept of **circular causality** that was contained in Bateson's work) and in places, in our experience, this blaming attitude can still be found today.

Recognising that blaming families for causing schizophrenia was at one time the prevailing attitude in psychiatric services and may still exist, current mental health workers' attitudes need to be taken into account (and influenced if necessary) as part of an initiative to promote family interventions in routine practice. Accessible material based on research findings (for example, Leff 1998; Smith and Velleman 2002) can be used to educate practitioners and enable them to understand their part in providing family work to all families in need. But in our experience, by far the most effective way to encourage workers to provide family interventions is for them to hear carers tell their stories. Carers who have reached a level of understanding about how to cope with psychosis are likely to be willing to take part in this process (Mohr *et al.* 2000) and benefit from knowing they are making a difference to the future provision of mental health services (Smith 2003).

Having established a mental health service's willingness to offer family work, there needs to be a managerial decision about the best ways to deliver it. Our suggestion is that each team (which may include workers from the voluntary sector that are funded to meet carers' needs) should have two or three members who are proficient in providing the interventions in practice. The rest of the team then need only develop sufficient skill and knowledge to recognise a family in need, be able to briefly explain what family work entails to a family and make appropriate, timely referrals.

There is a need for family workers to have access to adequate training and supervision, which means, in practice, we are suggesting three levels of competence (Smith 1999; Smith and Velleman 2002) as shown in Box 4.1. It is also worth remembering that although they will not directly deliver family work in practice it is often useful if mental health team managers can develop the Level 1 competence in order to provide knowledgeable support to those delivering the actual interventions.

Box 4.1 Levels of competence needed to deliver family work in routine practice

Level 1: Awareness of the intervention in order to recognise the need for family work, discuss it with families and make appropriate referrals. This is likely to include consultants, GPs, PCTs, voluntary agencies, in-patient staff working on acute units and all members of CMHTs, home treatment, Assertive Outreach (AO) teams or crisis resolution teams. This can be achieved by workers attending presentations and reading relevant journals or books.

Level 2: As above, plus an ability to offer family interventions. This could include any members of a CMHT, AO teams, rehabilitation units, voluntary organisations and residential care settings, and is equally applicable by any member of a multi-disciplinary mental health team. The necessary skills and knowledge can be attained by workers attending formal training courses or by apprenticeship, working alongside a skilled family worker.

Level 3: As above, plus an ability to teach family work skills and offer supervision pertinent to all aspects of family work in practice. This is appropriate to the few workers who wish to become specialists in family interventions. The **Thorn Diploma** is an example of suitable training for a practitioner at this level, but this in itself is not enough: it is in fact the consolidation of skills and knowledge through working with families that distinguishes Level 3 from Level 2.

Distinguishing these three levels means that staff can recognise the point at which they are competent to practice, and their responsibilities for service delivery at that level. A further important factor that distinguishes workers at Level 1 from Levels 2 and 3 is the length of time over which their regular input is likely to be possible. For example, we do not believe ward staff should provide formal family work if they are unable to protect the time devoted to it within their ward schedule, as it is counterproductive to arrange a meeting with a family only to cancel it at short notice due to competing demands on the ward staff's time. And we certainly do not condone ward staff providing family work to service users at home after their discharge from in-patient services, thus depleting the staff complement available to the remaining in-patients. However, we strongly support the development of reciprocal arrangements, whereby community workers deliver interventions to in-patients that promote and enhance continuity of care, as practised, for example, by the GRIP team in the Gloucestershire Partnership Trust (www.gripinitiative.org.uk). Nonetheless, in our experience some workers from in-patient facilities do achieve strong working alliances with families by challenging and adapting their ward schedules using the same collaborative problem-solving skills utilised within family work itself.

It is becoming apparent (Mohr *et al.* 2000) that the intervention required by families during a service user's in-patient treatment is not the same as the family work described in previous manuals (for example, Kuipers *et al.* 2002). We will explore this in further detail in Chapter 5 (When to Offer Family Work for Psychosis) and Chapter 6 (Where to do Family Work for Psychosis).

Not all mental health workers are suited to become family workers (Smith 1999) as there are personal qualities that family workers need to possess, including self-awareness and an ability to be 'approachable, purposeful, flexible and ordinary' (Gamble 2000, p.116). Moreover, even when workers have these attributes they can be forgotten when the workers find themselves in an unfamiliar situation, such as working with a whole family rather than the service user alone. We make this point to remind practitioners to nurture and have confidence in their personal qualities while developing the specific skills required to provide family interventions. It is our hope that this acknowledgement will help you and your co-worker to maintain the qualities highlighted by Gamble (2000) when you find yourselves under pressure, and to avoid the temptation to be over-assertive in an attempt to manage your own stress.

Much of the knowledge and many of the skills learned and used regularly by mental health workers within their practice elsewhere (including an array of counselling skills, medical knowledge, group work skills, case management experience and the vast knowledge that they have of the how the mental health system operates) are valuable to them as family workers. However, there is one particular skill that we feel is most useful that family workers need to acquire if they do not already have it. This is being able to use **Socratic questioning** to help individuals find their own answers, rather than looking to mental health workers to solve their problems.

In our integrated model of family work we advocate co-working. We realise that workers may not be familiar with this style of working, so we cover its principles and practice in detail in Chapter 7 (How to Prepare for Family Work Meetings). However, first, in order to identify potential family workers, it is important to explore and try to understand our fellow workers' beliefs, attitudes and knowledge. We urge you to take the time to consider these issues when identifying a co-worker with whom you will provide family interventions, as we have found this crucial point in deciding who should be involved in providing family work for psychosis is often overlooked, with workers gratefully accepting anybody who is willing to work with them. This can be a mistake if workers find out at a later date (possibly in front of the family with whom they are co-working) that they have a clash of personality or incompatible philosophical beliefs.

Identifying carers to participate in family work

Initially it is possible that family work may not include the service user, and indeed this may continue in the longer term. Nevertheless, it is important that the service user has given permission for family work to take place and their involvement encouraged throughout, as discussed in Chapter 7. On the rare occasions that a service user continues to refuse to have any part in the family work, carers may be supported by working through their own experiences and issues without the service user present. In such situations the family workers need to be careful not to inappropriately divulge confidential information about the service user and also to remain aware of the limitations of this approach, as we know that effective interventions include the service user in at least some of the family meetings (Fadden 1998; Vaughan *et al.* 1992). We therefore always work towards having the service user present at some stage in family work. However, at times, separate sessions without the service user may be offered to carers specifically. An example of when this would be appropriate would be to reaffirm the marital relationship between spouses and plan how they might spend time together, to consider their own needs without their son or daughter present. Equally, it may be useful for the service user to receive individual therapy alongside the family work. In such cases it is most helpful if the individual therapist is also one of the family workers, as it ensures that the lessons learned from the two interventions are integrated to maximise the benefits.

Summary

If we ask ourselves the question 'Who is family work appropriate for?', the answer will be 'Anyone who offers significant support to a service user.' The carer need not be related to the service user by birth or marriage, although in most cases we find ourselves offering family work to parents or spouses. However, it is equally applicable to staff working in supported lodgings, residential care settings or nursing homes. Indeed family interventions may be offered to any '**significant other**' identified by the service user, providing there is a 'significant' amount of face-to-face contact between them.

Family interventions may be offered by anyone who has had some appropriate training and can access family work supervision. This includes workers from statutory and voluntary mental health services as well as carers who feel ready to give formal support to others.

Key points

- Within our integrated family work model, the word 'family' is used in the widest sense of the word. For example, a close friend or staff within a residential setting can represent a service user's family.

- Our model of family work is a co-working model, so will be provided by two workers, at least one of whom will usually have had family work training. Both should be in receipt of supervision specific to this work.

- The service user's care coordinator should (in most cases) be one of the family workers. If he or she is not directly involved in the family interventions, the work will need to be integrated with other aspects of the service user's care plan, through regular communication between all workers in between family meetings, as well as formal care planning meetings.

- All mental health workers need to understand family work in order to recognise when to make an appropriate referral. Fewer workers need to be trained to deliver family interventions, thus involving all workers appropriately in providing family work in routine practice.

- Workers delivering family interventions will benefit from accessing practice supervision and/or training from a very experienced family worker who has the knowledge, skill and time to help them develop their practice.

- Family interventions may be provided by mental health workers from any discipline, as long as they have undertaken some relevant training (whether formal or informal) and are in receipt of family work supervision.

- Mental health workers from voluntary organisations are just as able to provide family interventions as workers employed by statutory services.

- Carers as well as mental health workers can be trained to deliver family interventions.

- When asked to evaluate the effectiveness of family interventions, carers comment on the qualities of the family worker (or in other words the interventionist) as well as the quality of the family interventions.

- Families that frequently contact staff for reassurance and/or help are likely to benefit from family work.

Recommended further reading

Bainbridge, M. (2002) 'Carers are People Too.' *Mental Health Today*, June, 24–27.

Fadden, G. (1998) 'Family Intervention.' In C. Brooker and J. Repper (eds) (2000) *Serious Mental Health Problems in the Community – Policy, Practice and Research.* London: Bailliere Tindall.

Gamble, C. and Brennan, G. (2000) 'Working with Families and Informal Carers.' In G. Gamble and G. Brennan (eds) *Working with Serious Mental Illness – A Practice Manual.* London: Bailliere Tindall.

Moore, E., Ball, R. and Kuipers, E. (1992) 'Expressed Emotion in Staff Working With the Long-Term Mentally Ill.' *British Journal of Psychiatry 161*, 802–808.

Smith, G. (1999) 'Linking Theory with Practice.' *Mental Health Care 3*, 4, 133–135.

Smith, G. and Velleman, R. (2002) 'Maintaining a Family Work for Psychosis Service by Recognising and Addressing the Barriers to Implementation.' *Journal of Mental Health 11*, 5, 471–479.

5

When to Offer Family
Work for Psychosis

Offering family work for psychosis

Ideally, all those caring for a mental health service user who has a diagnosis of severe mental illness would be offered family work. Realistically, however, not everyone wants it, there are constraints on resources and some groups may benefit more than others. So when might family work be offered to maximise its potential benefits?

Early recognition of a psychotic illness is important, as the longer the psychosis is left untreated, the longer the first and second hospital admissions are likely to be (Birchwood *et al.* 2000). This gives rise to a poorer quality of life for all family members and higher long-term health care costs. Families, if listened to (Smith 2003), can play an important part in this early recognition.

Having acknowledged the psychosis, intensive input during the first episode is beneficial (Goldstein, Rodnick and Evans 1978; Sainsbury Centre for Mental Health 2003). Between 10 and 25 per cent of people with psychosis commit suicide, with the greatest risk early on, especially within the first three years after diagnosis (Birchwood 2000), highlighting the need to support service users experiencing their first episode of psychosis. Family work at this stage may also reduce the early development of high expressed emotion (EE) and carer burden (Kuipers and Raune 2000). However, there appear to be particular ways that family interventions need to be offered to those coping with a first episode of psychosis (Addington and Burnett 2004) that you may need to consider if working in such situations.

Groups comprising individuals from various backgrounds who share a great deal of interest in the early stages of psychosis have produced guidelines that give the reasons why we should join with families coping with psychosis as early as possible. In Box 5.1 we have summarised those produced by the Initiative to Reduce the Impact of Schizophrenia (www.iris-initiative.org.uk) and the Early Psychosis Prevention and Intervention Centre (EPPIC 1997). This work with families should fit within the 'Early Psychosis Declaration' (WHO 2004) that describes the outcomes that those experiencing a first psychotic episode should expect to attain.

Box 5.1 Possible reasons to offer family interventions as soon as psychosis is suspected

It is useful to join families coping with psychosis at the earliest opportunity in order to:

- avoid conflict between the service user, carers and mental health service providers related to issues of confidentiality; if carers are involved in the service user's care from the start, then this sets a pattern in which there are open and honest channels of communication and information sharing
- encourage a combined and collaborative effort towards recovery from psychosis involving the service user, carer and mental health service providers
- minimise any disruption to the **family system**
- maximise and help to guide the coping strategies that the service user and carers are already developing
- minimise the risk of prolonged grief, stress, depression or high levels of burden that isolated carers are prone to develop
- reduce the likelihood of the service user becoming either dependent on or alienated from his or her family as a result of the psychosis
- help all members of the family to understand the illness and the possible treatments available for psychosis
- develop strategies to avert and/or cope with crises and respond to early warning signs (EWS) of a possible psychotic relapse, in an effort to facilitate relapse prevention and/or minimise the impact of a psychotic episode.

Although a clear diagnosis of psychosis may take some time, this need not delay family workers in providing help and support to both service users and carers trying to manage troublesome **signs and symptoms**. It is possible and valuable to focus family interventions at this point on the experience caused by the symptoms rather than a discussion or debate about the name of the illness.

Indeed, the use of the term schizophrenia too early can be 'misguided and incorrect' (SCMH 2003, p.15). Therefore, developing an understanding of what is happening for the family can be much more beneficial and helpful than agreeing upon a definitive diagnosis at this early stage. It has been shown that families are more willing to accept help when they are experiencing a crisis (Barrowclough and Tarrier 1997), so times of crisis are a crucial time for family workers to become involved and present themselves as a resource to the family (Gamble and Brennan 2000; Kuipers *et al.* 2002).

Furthermore, it may be that a crisis presents some mental health service providers with an opportunity for engaging with a family, as they are made aware of a problem when emergency services such as the police become involved. This most often occurs when violence ensues, as a family's attempts to cope on their own are overwhelmed or when families simply do not understand that the behaviours they are struggling with are symptoms of an illness. At such a dire stage even the most under-resourced mental health team is likely to recognise the needs of a family in this situation and offer to help them, where family intervention may not have been available before.

In our experience, carers who make frequent contacts to mental health services for reassurance or help, and also those who make complaints, can benefit from family work, although their need for help and support may not be articulated explicitly (particularly if carers do not understand the illness and therefore do not know what to ask for). However, by offering family work, service providers demonstrate their wish to properly understand the carer's issues, which may be the first step towards developing a collaborative relationship. This collaboration can then be deepened through the family work process itself, starting with the assessments described in Chapter 8 (How to Conduct Family Work Assessments), which can then inform an agreed action plan.

The National Institute for Clinical Excellence Guidelines for Schizophrenia (NICE 2002), which are also available in a version written in lay terms for the general public, and the Early Psychosis Declaration (WHO 2004) both highlight the benefits of family work. As families become more aware of services that can be available through these types of publication, then more requests from carers for family interventions are likely to be forthcoming. Mental health service providers need to prepare themselves for these requests, as in our experience (Smith and Velleman 2002) once a family has identified a need for family work it should be offered within two to three weeks or the risk of non-engagement and dissatisfaction is high.

None of the suggestions above excludes anyone from asking for family work at any time, even if they are not identified within any of these high-risk groups. Neither should carers who refuse the initial offer of family work be excluded (Budd and Hughes 1997). It could be, for those that decline, that the time is not right for intervention, but as this may change, carers should be made aware that family work can be offered again. They should also understand that they could request it for themselves, if they feel the need at some point in the future. Alternatively, it may be possible to work with part of the family system in order to gain their trust and provide some help, with the possibility that others will join the meetings at a later date. However, participating in family work can never be made compulsory, as it needs to be a collaborative endeavour and therefore cannot be forced.

Engaging families on in-patient units

Family work in the context of in-patient settings is not well understood. (Glick *et al.* 1993; McCann and Bowers 2005), but this does not mean it should not be attempted. Nevertheless, how best to use family work within an in-patient unit needs careful consideration given that the length of the admission is often brief or undefined, which makes planning ongoing family meetings difficult. Traditionally wards have been busy environments in which staff face immediate competing demands for their time, needing to balance the needs of individuals with those of the ward community as a whole (McCann and Bowers 2005). This has made offering interventions such as family work, which need to be organised some days in advance, difficult to operationalise.

The lack of opportunity to deliver evidence-based family interventions has, in our experience, left ward staff feeling they have nothing to offer, mirroring the position of community mental health workers a decade ago (Winefield and Burnett 1996) before family work training was so widely available. However, our evolving understanding of the needs of carers during the service user's in-patient treatment (Mohr *et al.* 2000) has helped us and carers develop and provide appropriate help at this stage (see www.carershelpcarers.org.uk).

Carers frequently tell us that seeing a loved one (the service user) admitted to an in-patient unit leaves them feeling both relieved and desolate, especially when it is a first admission. We recognise that a detailed carers' pack, such as the one available from the Avon and Wiltshire Mental Health Partnership NHS Trust (AWP), would probably be overwhelming at this point. Nonetheless carers need some information to enable them to maintain contact with the service user and those caring for him or her. With this in mind Lu Duhig, working for AWP, devised a form called 'Who Can Help Me?' (shown in Appendix 5), which is given to carers as soon as is practically possible. Carers report that this pre-prepared sheet demonstrates to them that the in-patient staff are aware of their needs, and this does much to engender a good working relationship between themselves, the service user and the mental health service providers. We therefore recommend that you encourage the use of such a form by the wards in your locality.

Reframing a crisis as an opportunity for change

A crisis is frequently a manifestation that a service user and/or carer has been overwhelmed by the problems associated with psychosis or that their previous coping strategies have ceased to be effective. A crisis can, therefore, be **reframed** as an opportunity to try to do things differently, although obviously this message needs to be delivered with a great deal of sensitivity when speaking to distressed carers or service users. So you should always clearly acknowledge the carer's position, to show that you have heard and appreciate his or her struggles.

Often we find that, when faced with a crisis, carers who have previously been dismissive become willing to discuss family interventions and possibly engage in a formal carers' assessment (Carers Recognition and Services Act 1995; DH 1999) to properly establish their problems, strengths and needs, and discuss new ways of coping. Using a structured framework such as the Care Programme Approach (DH 1990a, 1990b), as discussed in Chapter 4 (Who is Involved in Family Work for Psychosis?), is important to ensure that the carer's needs and the service user's needs are considered and attended to within a coherent overall care plan in which all those involved are clear about their roles and responsibilities. We have included a suggestion of how to structure an initial carer's assessment in Appendix 6 (as used in the Avon and Wiltshire Mental Health Partnership NHS Trust), having found that this structure helps devise a carer's care plan in response to the assessed needs. However, many carers seem to prefer the assessment itself to appear quite informal, so the use of the form itself may not always be appropriate, taking brief notes is almost always acceptable.

Getting started

Referrals

In order that carers are offered intervention at a time that is most helpful to them, it may be useful for mental health service providers to devise a system for managing the referral process. This can be facilitated by a clear referral form (such as the example provided in Appendix 6, as used in the Avon and Wiltshire Mental Health Partnership NHS Trust). The completed form is then passed on to a person with a coordinating role (Smith and Velleman 2002), who can access workers that are in a position to provide family work if it is required.

In our experience timing is important, regardless of whether the family is in crisis or they are ready to accept help for other reasons. A coordinated referral process reduces the likelihood of families having to wait too long (which risks the point for most fruitful engagement being missed).

A system that includes a coordinator can begin to pave the way for the development of mental health services that accept family work as a part of their everyday practice, thereby offering intervention to all families in need. This coordinating role should also maintain an awareness of any mismatch between demand for family work and the availability of resources to provide it, again to avoid families having to wait more than two or three weeks once their need for family intervention has been acknowledged. Structure within a flexible framework is the essence of this referral and allocation process.

Following the referral we find it is always worth one or both of the family workers trying to meet the service user and carers to discuss issues face to face. A written overview of the family work process (shown in Appendix 3) may help the family members gain a better understanding of what the intervention is likely to involve, which helps them to make an informed choice about whether to engage or not.

At first, our work with families may begin in a rather haphazard fashion. This is to be expected, but nonetheless, workers need to be aware of their sense of purpose: to meet with the family and introduce the concept of family work, as described within Chapter 1 (Introduction). Worthy of note is that it is often important for family workers not to do too much too soon. Instead, we should listen, acknowledge and assess the carer's coping strategies, the level of burden expressed and any boundary issues, which helps us to gain the necessary awareness of their strengths and needs. The use of **active listening skills** is essential to ascertain the appropriateness of family work and to avoid making assumptions about the need for intervention. This means paying attention not only to what is said, but also to any non-verbal cues and possible avoidance of discussing particular subjects. Family workers need to feel grounded and safe themselves, with sufficient knowledge, to enable them to avoid imposing control onto the family system. Training and supervision are vital in promoting family workers' sense of security, which they can then transmit to the service user and carers.

We suggest that students learning family work skills should work initially (if possible) with a family that appears to have uncomplicated needs, to allow new family workers to develop and consolidate their skills through a relatively straightforward experience before tackling more complex issues. However, the level of complexity may not always be possible to gauge prior to meeting carers. Therefore, ongoing family work supervision needs to be used to provide support and guidance within a structured framework, to ensure that workers do not become overwhelmed by the experiences and needs of carers and service users.

When to engage in family work: why now?

When some doubt exists about the appropriateness of family work, it is often worth asking the question 'Why now?' in response to a potential referral. In Box 5.2 we have listed some of the possible answers to this question.

Box 5.2 Reasons to offer family interventions

Family work should be offered when:

- the need for family work is identified within the Care Programme Approach (DH 1990a, 1990b) or other care planning framework
- the service user finds it difficult to engage with mental health services and this is placing a burden on carers or putting them at risk
- there is conflict between the service user, the carer and/or mental health workers
- emergency services have been called recently to help the family deal with a crisis or violent incident
- the service user and/or carer is socially isolated
- one or more family members are experiencing a problem associated with psychosis that is impacting on other family members
- the service user has experienced a recent psychotic relapse or is experiencing EWS of an impending relapse
- intolerance and stress among those with whom the service user lives has increased
- the service user and/or carer is vulnerable to abuse
- this is the first diagnosis of psychosis
- the service user has experienced multiple psychotic relapses
- any family requests it.

Increasing the likelihood of engaging families

Often carers request information when a diagnosis of psychosis is first made, or a relapse of the psychosis brings the service user in to hospital. It is important for all mental health workers to be aware of the potential benefits of family work at such points of contact, as described in Chapter 4 (Who is Involved in Family Work for Psychosis?), so that carers are not given information out of context. It appears that when this does happen it is common for carers then to refuse family work when it is offered later, on the grounds that they have already received what they wanted in terms of information (although this information may well not be all that they needed). Introducing the whole concept of family work at this early stage, and if possible introducing the family workers too, capitalises on the family's readiness to engage.

Summary

It is important to offer family interventions as soon as psychosis is suspected. If it has not already been accepted family work should be offered again when a service user's mental illness is given a firm diagnosis and/or if a crisis occurs.

Family members may not always be ready to accept family intervention as soon as the mental health workers involved recognise that it might be beneficial. If the intervention is refused it is still possible for mental health workers to adopt a collaborative stance with carers and service users, whereby family work can successfully be offered at some point in the future.

Key points

- Family work should be offered at the earliest opportunity.
- Families are probably most open to family intervention at times of crisis or change.
- When families request practical help or information they should be offered family intervention, not just what they are asking for; information alone, for example, is unlikely to reduce psychotic relapse rates.
- In complex situations, such as when there is police involvement or the use of the Mental Health Act 1983, it is good practice to offer family work.
- A service user's in-patient admission may prompt mental health service providers to offer family work. However, carers and service users may not be ready to accept it immediately.
- Families who refuse family work initially may well accept it at a later date, if it is offered again.
- Families who refuse family work should not be discriminated against; workers should always try to work collaboratively with service users and carers.

Recommended further reading

Addington, J. and Burnett, P. (2004) 'Working with Families in the Early Stages of Psychosis.' In J. Gleeson and P. McGorry (eds) *Psychological Interventions in Early Psychosis.* Chichester: Wiley & Sons.

Early Psychosis Prevention and Intervention Centre (1997) *Working with Families in Early Psychosis.* Victoria: EPPIC.

Goldstein, M., Rodnick, E. and Evans, J. (1978) 'Drug and Family Therapy in the Aftercare of Acute Schizophrenia.' *Archives of General Psychiatry 35*, 1169–77.

Gamble, C. and Brennan, G. (2000) 'Working with Families and Informal Carers.' In C. Gamble and G. Brennan (eds) *Working with Serious Mental Illness. A Manual for Clinical Practice.* London: Bailliere Tindall.

Kuipers, E. and Raune, D. (2000) 'The Early Detection of Expressed Emotion and Burden in Families of First-Onset Psychosis.' In M. Birchwood, D. Fowler and C. Jackson (eds) *Early Intervention in Psychosis. A Guide to Concepts, Evidence and Interventions.* Chichester: Wiley & Sons.

Kuipers, L., Leff, J. and Lam, D. (2002) *Family Work for Schizophrenia. A Practical Guide* (2nd edn). London: Gaskell.

Macmillan, F. and Shiers, D. (2000) "The IRIS Programme." In M. Birchwood, D. Fowler and C. Jackson (eds) *Early Intervention in Psychosis. A Guide to Concepts, Evidence and Interventions.* Chichester: Wiley & Sons.

McCann, E. and Bowers, L. (2005) 'Training in Cognitive Behavioural Interventions on Acute Psychiatric Wards.' *Journal of Psychiatric and Mental Health Nursing 12*, 215–222.

National Institute for Clinical Excellence (NICE) (2002) *Schizophrenia: Core Interventions in the Treatment and Management of Schizophrenia in Primary and Secondary Care.* London: NICE Guideline.

World Health Organization (2004) *Early Psychosis Declaration.* Geneva: World Health Organisation.

Recommended web-based resource

www.iris-initiative.org.uk Early Intervention in Psychosis: Clinical Guidelines and Service Frameworks and Tool Kit.

6

Where to do Family
Work for Psychosis

Choosing a venue

Family work may be offered within a range of different settings by a number of mental health service providers. We argue that Level 1 competence in family work, as described in Chapter 4 (Who is Involved in Family Work for Psychosis?), should be part of the core skills of all mental health workers (Brooker and Brabban 2003), so that wherever they are employed and however mental health services are configured the need for family work can be recognised. We also suggest that two or three team members acquire Level 2 competence, as described in Chapter 4, so that family work may be offered within community mental health teams, early intervention teams, assertive outreach teams, forensic units, substance misuse services, any residential settings, and so on. This generalised awareness can ensure that collaborative contact is made with carers when a service user is in receipt of care from in-patient services, crisis resolution or home treatment teams.

How family work is practised may be slightly different according to the context of the various service settings in which it is delivered, but this should not hamper the continuation or completion of the family work if the service user moves from one setting to another. This means all mental health workers, as we have stated before, should have an overall understanding of what family work is (known as Level 1 competence), and how and where it can best be facilitated. This could include workers from voluntary organisations, such as **Rethink**, and Local Authority mental health care facilities.

Voluntary organisations that are funded to meet carers' needs may also train their workers to achieve Level 2 competence, so that they can provide family interventions. In such cases we recommend that these workers co-work with a family worker from statutory services in order to model partnership working and ensure that the family interventions are reviewed within the context of the service user's overall care plan (McFarlane *et al.* 1995). The venue for the work will then be chosen accordingly to meet the family's needs.

In reality, most family work is done in the service user's family home. The rationale for this is that people are most forthcoming in a non-threatening, natural setting and, in this environment, they can be encouraged to converse freely without any insinuation that there are right and wrong responses. It has been found that this is not always the case in a clinic setting, as service users and carers there may try to give a particular response in order to please the practitioner (Porter 1996).

However, for some service users, carers or other family members who do not class themselves as carers directly, the family home may be threatening or just not the best place to meet, so any alternative that affords sufficient privacy may be chosen. In such cases the family meetings may be offered at other venues, such as those listed in Box 6.1.

Box 6.1 Possible venues (other than the family home) for family interventions

As an alternative to the family home, family intervention may be provided in:

- the service user's home, if different from the carer's
- a residential care home, hostel or supported lodgings
- an in-patient unit
- a mental health day hospital, a day centre or resource centre
- any primary health care setting
- CMHT meeting room.

It is important to be flexible and think about how and why the particular venue has been chosen, as this may be critical to whether or not the family is able to get together. For example, the ward may be the most appropriate venue if the service user is an in-patient still experiencing florid symptoms of psychosis. Alternatively, a service user who is an in-patient, but well on the way to recovery, may be encouraged to go on home leave in order to attend family meetings and plan for discharge. There may be other circumstances where it is more appropriate to meet on neutral ground if such a place can be found, and this will need to be negotiated with the service user and carers. In our experience this is most often necessary if aggression or violence has been a feature of the service user's psychosis. However, it is sometimes the case that meeting in the carer's home can be instrumental in helping the service user integrate back into the **family system**.

When working with service users experiencing their first episode of psychosis there is a particular need for a responsive, user-friendly service to reduce the fear and stigma associated with mental health services (Macmillan and Shiers 2000). Good links between the primary health care team and mental health facilities may help to reduce the stigma of needing to use mental services, as perceived by many first-time service users and encourage them to engage fully in the family work process and the rest of their care plan.

Managing the environment in which family meetings take place

The environment where the family meetings take place, whether it is on the premises of mental health services, other services or in the family home, requires consideration about how best to use the working space. As a family worker you will need to think about how the family members communicate with each other, including who sits close to whom and where your co-worker will sit. If you have control over the environment you can arrange the seating as you require and politely show those attending the meeting to their seats. However, in a family home or the home of the service user this may be more difficult to achieve and you may not have so much flexibility.

If the meeting is to take place in the family home, we recommend that, at the first family meeting after you have completed the initial assessments, you begin by asking where people usually sit and then find the best place for you and your co-worker to position yourselves. During this meeting you should be mindful how family members communicate with each other from these places, as this can be a rich source of information about their communication skills and family patterns of communicating. For example, some seating arrangements can block individuals' views of one other and therefore change the quality of their communication. This can become a point of discussion either with the family at the time when you notice it or at a later date if you feel this would be likely to be useful. You and your co-worker should certainly consider it when preparing for the next and subsequent meetings.

If poor communication is perceived as an issue that requires intervention you may request that you all try an experiment with the seating arrangements, if this is a practical option, to possibly help promote clearer interaction. However, in most cases you need to feel that you have sufficiently engaged the family and developed a good rapport before making such suggestions. These experiments are usually most fruitful if the service user and carers are aware of what you as family workers are thinking and trying to achieve, as this openness enables them to give more informative feedback and make further suggestions. This can also serve as an early example for the family that family work truly is a collaborative endeavour and that the workers are not there (as they may have suspected or feared) to quietly judge them.

While there are obvious advantages to meeting in the family's home there might be some disadvantages (such as someone answering the phone or repeatedly offering refreshments) that make the meetings feel quite disjointed. If this is the case it is useful for family workers to remember that what they are experiencing could mirror the chaotic ways the family usually gets together. It may be that meeting all together is an unusual event at which they are unpractised, or could represent one or more family members finding the process uncomfortable (or even painful) and that the distractions serve as a welcome relief. In such instances it may be useful to switch to using mental health service premises, in order to model for the family how to limit distractions and make explicit the benefits that can be achieved when the time and space for family work are protected. Nevertheless, it is important that, ultimately, the family members start to make use of the skills learned through family work with their own environment, if they are going to continue to use them when the family workers are no longer present (Falloon *et al.* 1993).

Other sources of distraction within the family home are more minor and can be seen as normal social practices (Kuipers *et al.* 2002), such as making a cup of tea when workers arrive, smoking cigarettes, intrusions by family pets, or even having the television or radio on. These still need to be managed so that they do not interfere with the family work process. However, family workers must take care to observe appropriate customs when working with families from particular cultural backgrounds, as failure to do so is likely to lead to the worker's help being rejected; so, for example, workers must not presume that all offers of food constitute a distraction.

Whatever the distractions, you and your co-worker will need to discuss them with each other when planning for family meetings and decide how you can respectfully approach the subject (if necessary) with the family. Indeed, these practical aspects of meeting are likely to prove valuable in helping the family to begin to work together to solve problems, and can make real the purpose of the collaboratively agreed **ground rules**, as described in Chapter 7 (How to Prepare for Family Work Meetings).

Summary

Family work may take place in many different places. All venues have potential advantages and disadvantages, which should be considered before the most suitable venue is chosen. However, the long-term goals of the family meeting includes that it should occur in a place where family members will continue to meet when family work has ceased, in order to maximise the likelihood that they will adopt the lessons learned though family intervention in their day-to-day lives.

Key points

- Family work can be offered within a wide range of settings and services.
- Flexibility regarding the family work venue may facilitate the intervention actually taking place.
- There may be disadvantages and advantages to meeting at home, or in a mental health service environment.
- There should be an explicit rationale for the chosen venue.
- The place where family work takes place should be accessible to all those invited to get together.
- Co-workers need to think carefully about how they will use the physical space provided and should not be afraid to move furniture (with permission) in order to aid the process.

Recommended further reading

Kuipers, L., Leff, J. and Lam, D. (2002) *Family Work for Schizophrenia. A Practical Guide* (2nd edn). London: Gaskell.

Section 2

Delivering Family Work for Psychosis

7

How to Prepare for Family Work Meetings

How family work begins

We will start this chapter with an overview of the family work process, shown in Figure 7.1, to serve as a reminder of how family interventions may progress.

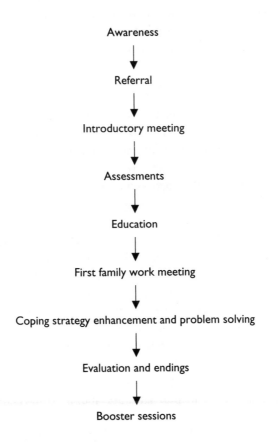

Figure 7.1 A brief overview of the family work process

Our family work flowchart (of which a more detailed version can be found as Figure 2.1 in Chapter 2 (What is Family Work for Psychosis?) is offered as a guide to family workers, service users and carers, to help them to visualise the whole family work process; a descriptive version without acronyms can be found in Appendix 3. As we have said before, it is not meant to be prescriptive and you may indeed need to begin your work with a family at any point in the process charted here. For example, members of a family may be in need of immediate help to communicate with each other more effectively, in order to resolve a problem that has become a focus for their attention, before they can work together in the education sessions. To rigidly follow the flowchart in such circumstances would be inappropriate and could lead carers to disengage, as it is unlikely that they would gain much benefit from the early family meetings if they felt their concerns were not adequately addressed. What will become apparent from working with our flowchart is that if you start at a point other than the beginning, then you will miss what comes before and will need to return to these points. However, for ease of explaining how to work with families within this chapter, we will follow the linear flow of the chart, as shown in Figure 7.1.

Co-working

Before we begin to explore the detail of how to provide the various components of family work, we will first discuss how family workers need to prepare themselves to deliver family interventions in practice alongside a co-worker. When providing family work for psychosis there are particular issues that relate to co-working, including modelling behaviours, developing a trusting relationship, communication, forming alliances, planning family meetings and supporting one another within meetings (Kuipers *et al.* 2002). These important elements of family interventions could not be undertaken so effectively and/or could be overwhelming for a single practitioner working with families. Moreover, in order to manage the process a worker forced to work alone would be likely to adopt a more strictly behavioural approach that would not permit family members to discuss their feelings (Falloon *et al.* 1984). Therefore, we believe that co-working is not a luxury but essential to our integrated model of family work.

Modelling is the word we use for demonstrating to others the behaviours and attitudes of one or more people that are likely to lead to particular responses in another. Through co-working the family workers have opportunities to explicitly model both helpful and unhelpful attitudes and/or behaviours, often with humour, to help service users and carers explore the ways they communicate (both verbally and non-verbally) with each other. By being 'approachable' and 'ordinary' (Gamble 2000, p.116) workers can show that, although they do not always get things perfectly right, they are still able to resolve differences of opinion without criticising one another or being hostile. So if you disagree or are not sure of what your co-worker means during a family meeting, you can model negotiating skills, showing how to work together and how you can capitalise on elements from each other's different points of view.

Within a family meeting co-workers can sometimes purposefully try to resolve an issue that the family is struggling with by adopting the positions of those expressing differing views, while modelling acceptance of each other, to demonstrate particular communication skills. However, family workers must resist the temptation to repeatedly show the family how to solve problems by merely providing solutions, rather than making explicit the structured approach that facilitates their effective problem solving. Our suggested problem-solving framework is described fully in Chapter 10 (How to Promote Recovery Through Family Work).

Trust between the workers is vital when co-working, respecting each other's judgement and co-operating with one another, both within the family meetings themselves and when planning them. This must not be a competitive relationship. Having achieved this trust, workers generally find co-working very comfortable and comforting. This is particularly apparent at those moments when one family worker becomes unsure or loses confidence in the point he or she was trying to make; the trusting relationship creates a safe environment in which your co-worker can take over the lead worker role if necessary, while you collect your thoughts.

Yet sometimes you and your co-worker may have negative feelings towards each other, which (if they occur) will generally need to be addressed immediately after the meeting during which those feelings arose, within the time you have set aside to debrief. It is likely that you will most quickly recreate a positive working alliance by being very specific about your feelings, highlighting if you can the exact action or interaction that provoked the negative response (just as we encourage family members to do). However, if there are ongoing issues that you cannot resolve between yourselves, we suggest you discuss them within supervision as soon as possible. This may even necessitate calling your supervisor to request some help before your next family meeting, if this is due to take place before the next planned supervision session. Although this may feel awkward at the time, in our experience it is much less uncomfortable than trying to provide family interventions with a co-worker with whom you have some unresolved interpersonal issues.

Through family interventions it is possible for workers to form creative therapeutic alliances with various members of a family, possibly to strengthen the voice of a service user who seems to find it difficult to express their point of view. It can also be a means to give support to a carer who is perceived by the workers to be taken little notice of, through one worker aligning themselves to what that carer is saying, re-enforcing his or her influence, while the co-worker helps other family members to respond actively. Alliances may also be used to work with and separate members of the family to enforce generational boundaries (Kuipers *et al.* 2002), if, for example, the care needed by the service user is making it difficult for his or her parents to spend any time alone together. Before initiating this type of intervention, however, it first needs to be discussed between the co-workers, to ensure they are in agreement about its appropriateness with a shared plan for how the alliance should be developed.

It is recommended that co-workers should be flexible in their alliances, so that service users and/or carers are not left with the impression that only one worker understands them. Therefore, co-workers may find that they need to alternate their alliances with different family members from meeting to meeting, or actually within a single family meeting. Again, discussing these issues when planning family meetings ensures that co-workers are taking the roles mindfully for a particular purpose, so that their impact can be discussed in supervision and evaluated.

A most important aspect of co-working is the time devoted to planning the family meetings themselves (especially when it is a new co-working relationship). This planning provides an opportunity for workers to meet to discuss their own abilities, strengths, knowledge, experience, attitudes and creative ideas. In order to get together in this way you will first need to understand something of each other's specific knowledge and experience of family work. Indeed, we suggest that, when planning to co-work with another mental health practitioner, you discuss your understandings of the concept of family work, as a means of judging whether or not you are in accord and feel you would work well together.

Having developed a shared concept of family work, co-workers are ready to accept a referral and arrange initial meetings with the family members concerned. At this point co-workers need to discuss what they each already know of the service user and carers, and whether there are actual or potential blocks to their working collaboratively with any family members.

Before any family meeting you and your co-worker need to agree some of the content of the meeting, formulate some joint aims and devise a provisional plan of how these may be achieved. You also need to determine how to organise the running of each family meeting by deciding what functions you will each perform. This will include who will start the opening conversation and who will take the lead in gathering and exploring issues and concerns in order to decide what the business of the meeting should be. It is also useful to decide who will actually write down the agenda, who will keep the focus on that agenda and how the meeting will be recorded. And we urge you not to forget that service users and carers can often very usefully take on the task of making notes during the family meeting, as well as writing them up fully afterwards and distributing them to all concerned. Moreover, this can be a good way to include a family member who is reluctant to speak much during the actual meetings (Falloon *et al.* 1984), giving him or her a means to demonstrate a commitment to the process.

Advantages of co-working

In Box 7.1 we have summarised the advantages of co-working that we have both experienced in our own practice and heard described by our students and **supervisees**.

Box 7.1 Possible advantages of co-working

- Family members and workers feeling physically safer.

- Workers are less likely to be overwhelmed by the scope of a whole family's needs; between them the workers are also more likely to be able to give sufficient attention to each family member.

- The workload can be shared when conducting the initial assessments, liaising with other colleagues or agencies.

- An opportunity for modelling different ways of communicating, is offered including positive resolutions to differences of opinion.

- Co-workers themselves find it supportive; if one gets stuck then the other is immediately present and can often work out a way forward.

- It provides a means to integrate different professional approaches in a single intervention.

- The possibility for workers to align themselves with different family members to influence relationships and interactions within the family.

- Issues are addressed that it would be difficult for a single worker to manage alone; it is likely to offer a means to tackle deeply emotive issues, so can be more quickly effective and therefore increase the cost efficiency of family work.

- One worker keeps the process on course by sticking to the agenda, while the co-worker concentrates on the content of what is being said and clarifying individuals' meanings; this increases the likelihood that any misunderstandings and/or

---

evidence of disengagement, as well as opportunities, will be noticed.

- Workers can plan meetings together and challenge each other if they think particular issues are being avoided.
- It helps each individual and the family to come back to the agreed agenda and keeping to time, and refocus the meeting if the discussion goes off at a tangent that appears less relevant than the scheduled business; if the new item is more relevant, then one worker can make sure the agenda is formally adjusted (rather than letting the meeting informally change direction), while the other attends to the new topic's emotional content.

Disadvantages of co-working

Although co-workers can be a tremendous support for each other during family work, there can nonetheless be disadvantages to co-working. We have listed some of the potential problems that we have come across in Box 7.2, in order to encourage you and your co-worker to consider them. Within each point we have also added some suggestions to reduce the risk that they arise in your practice.

Box 7.2 Possible disadvantages of co-working

Coordinating diaries
Most mental health workers and many carers have extraordinarily busy schedules within both their professional and personal lives; this needs to be respected when working with families, as well as when co-working. Therefore the precise nature of the commitment to regular meetings needs to be discussed realistically when bringing a number of potentially competing demands together, with neither the workers' nor an individual family member's needs taking precedence. Being creative about how meetings can happen, being clear about the resources available, using the time together constructively, being respectful and being flexible will all open up the possibilities for doing successful family work. A **ground rule** that applies to cancelling family meetings due to other commitments may be helpful too.

Threatening in a small family

If the family at the meetings comprises only the service user and one carer, then two workers may seem overwhelming. The workers will need to be sensitive about this by being aware of the power of their own presence, to try to ensure the family is not uncomfortable.

Different ways of working

Different professional backgrounds and/or philosophies do not have to be a disadvantage, as long as both workers can agree on the aims of family work and respect each other enough to work together. Then, in meetings, if there is a misunderstanding or difference of opinion the workers can model how to come to an amicable agreement or compromise. It is not acceptable if any differences lead to behaviours that leak into family meetings and/or interfere with the process.

Labour intensive

A co-working model of family work for psychosis is sometimes mistakenly seen as too expensive to be offered within routine practice. However, an economic analysis as described in Chapter 3 (Why Offer Family Work for Psychosis?), has shown that family interventions are cost effective even when the cost of training workers is added in to the calculation. Family workers should therefore feel able to defend the practice of co-working against this criticism and avoid any pressure to work alone with families.

Complex conflicts and dynamics

In some mental health teams there can be competition between therapists providing different types of therapy, which can sometimes get in the way of service users being offered the best treatment at the optimum time. Family workers are urged to avoid competitive discussions, but instead make use of good practice guidelines (NICE 2002), the National Service Framework for Mental Health (DH 1999), their organisation's practice governance systems, and so on, to support their practice.

Splitting

In some cases family workers may experience a service user's or carer's communication and/or behaviour differently from their co-worker, with one feeling sympathy, the other antipathy. This must be managed through supervision and not acted out within family meetings. Alternatively, co-workers may experience family members trying to come between them. Once again this will probably need to be explored within supervision, preferably through the use of role-play.

Choosing a co-worker

We have already described something of the qualities needed in a family worker within Chapter 4 (Who is Involved in Family Work for Psychosis?), so in this section we will not discuss again who may become a family worker, but instead concentrate on how you should go about choosing a co-worker.

Co-working within family interventions does not happen automatically, just because two workers come together for an apparently common purpose; there may in fact be some personal issues or differing styles of approach that are not compatible and make it impossible for two mental health workers to co-work. It is best to discover this as soon as possible, preferably before you meet the family with whom you intend to work together for the first time. So before entering a co-working relationship, it is important for you to examine your own beliefs, attitudes and knowledge and those of the other worker, which will enable you to consider how you and your potential co-worker could operate together. For example, how would you address an issue such as your co-worker being a more experienced mental health worker than you, while you have more experience of providing family work in practice? It is also worth considering how you might work with conflict or **collusion**.

In our experience, some understanding and respect for one another as people as well as practitioners aids the construction of a cohesive co-working relationship. Indeed, the qualities of good co-workers may be similar to those of carers who show a lack of high expressed emotion (EE) characteristics, as successful family workers create a low-EE response (Leff and Vaughn 1985). This allows them to help create an environment (in part due to their positive working alliance as co-workers) that is calm and objective. By working in partnership, co-workers can assist each other to adapt appropriately to the varied situations in which they find themselves working, bringing with them realistic expectations that aid the family in learning to cope more effectively with psychosis. The workers' style is neither intrusive nor confrontational, and has within it a considerable amount of empathy with what the family is experiencing. These characteristics are also valuable when negotiating the formation of a co-working relationship.

The service user's care coordinator will probably have a good knowledge of the service user; he or she may also be a family worker. In such cases it is usual for the care coordinator to become one of the co-workers in order to use their prior knowledge to inform the family intervention. However, the care coordinator may not be a trained family worker, which leaves a couple of options: it may still be appropriate for the care coordinator to become one of the co-workers, learning the necessary skills through apprenticeship by working alongside a skilled family worker; alternatively, it may be more useful to bring in two new workers to co-work with the family, particularly if there is a possibility that the service user is unlikely to engage in family interventions initially, and involving the care coordinator in this could precipitate disengagement from all mental health services. When discussing the potential for co-working with the care coordinator in this situation it is useful to ensure that he or she understands what is required (particularly in terms of the desirable personal qualities described in Chapter 4), plus embracing our suggested precautions before a co-working agreement is reached.

Skills and competences required to provide family work in practice

The Family Work Skills Checklist (FWSC), which is included here as Appendix 8, is used to develop and monitor the skills required by family workers in practice by many **Thorn Diploma** courses (Baguley *et al.* 2000) around the country, including our own that runs at the University of Gloucestershire. This scale, devised by Devane and colleagues (1998), has been shown to have good **inter-rater reliability** and to date we know of no better tool to serve its purpose.

The items within the FWSC relate to the technical skills and competences of both the lead family worker and the co-worker, as these roles are differentiated for training purposes. However, in practice co-workers are likely to alternate between taking the lead and offering co-worker support within a single session, so both workers will display a number of the skills and competences throughout any given family meeting.

The competences listed in the FWSC include: interpersonal skills, understanding, agenda setting, negotiating style, controlling the session, handling expressed emotion, and both giving and receiving feedback. The co-worker skills specifically include: evidence of preparation, sharing tasks, elaborating the other worker's statements, modelling conflict resolution without criticism or hostility, and balancing alliances. These must be performed in a way that supports the lead worker's position and never undermines it. The technical skills include: providing information about diagnosis with particular reference to the service user, encouraging clear communication, and facilitating the use of all the components of a structured approach to problem solving.

We find that, in order to demonstrate competence in practice, a family worker should generally aim to include at least two of the options listed in each section of the FWSC within any family meeting, accepting that some sections will at times be non-applicable if the aspect of intervention to which they refer is not due to be covered in that particular meeting. Taping meetings (with the informed consent of those involved, including the care coordinator if he or she is not one of the family workers) will allow workers to accurately review the meeting together as well as share it with others during their formal practice supervision.

Supervision

Supervision is now accepted as an essential component of good clinical practice among all professional groups (Milne and James 2000), although some managers and practitioners still do not afford it sufficient priority. This can make it difficult for workers to allocate time for supervision within busy schedules and, even when it is scheduled, in our experience supervision is often the thing that is sacrificed if an emergency arises. We therefore feel compelled to stress the importance of supervision in family work and encourage you and your co-worker to use it productively (Blocher 1983). Indeed, a supervision group's perspective has often helped us to make progress in situations where we and the family with whom we were working have felt stuck. Without the benefit of supervision we are sure that the overall number of family meetings would have been extended in many cases, thereby increasing the overall cost of family work. From this we assert that supervision is cost effective and that it is a false economy on the part of managers to limit mental health workers' access to it.

The feedback received by a family worker on her or his contribution to a family meeting (whether this is from their co-worker, supervisor and/or other family workers) should both highlight what appeared to go well and according to plan, as well as identify areas for development. Often as mental health workers we tend to focus on the latter, rather than accept a balanced reflection that celebrates successes too. Moreover, we may need to practise noticing for ourselves what we do well, so that we develop good habits that will enable us to give positive feed-back to service users and carers, as well as our colleagues.

For family work we recommend group supervision: in groups supervisees can not only share their experiences, but also group members can provide a ready-made 'family' to take part in role-play scenarios, helping each other to examine and try to understand difficulties from a range of perspectives, develop further skills and continue to explore the intricacies of co-working (Liese and Beck 1997). We recognise that partaking in role-play situations may be uncomfortable at first, as can taping family meetings and listening to the tapes initially. However, the learning from these media can be so great and lasting that we urge you to try them; a training course or within peer group supervision may offer the necessary safe environment in which to start. As we were taught: practice makes perfect – well almost!

In Box 7.3 we show that there is a strong comparison between a family work meeting and group supervision session, demonstrating that a skilled family worker is able to run a peer supervision group for those practising family interventions. Nonetheless, we recommend developing some family workers to the Level 3 competence described in Chapter 4, as it is almost always valuable for a supervision group to be facilitated by a worker with a well-developed theoretical understanding of family interventions plus significant practice experience. And we have found that the most useful supervisors are those who are still actively practising family work, not those who have developed an interest but no longer work with families.

Box 7.3 Comparison of family work and supervision

Family work meeting	*Supervision session*
Begins by setting a collaborative agenda.	Begins by setting a collaborative agenda.
Prioritises items on agenda, with participants asking for time to be devoted to their issue.	Prioritises items on agenda, with workers bidding for time to be allocated to their issue.
Includes an update from previous meetings that links to the current meeting's agenda.	Includes an update from previous sessions that link to the current session's agenda.
Is an opportunity to reflect and explore interpersonal issues.	Is an opportunity to reflect back feelings and for interpersonal processes to be explored.
Is a collaborative process throughout.	Should be a collaborative process throughout.
Uses ground rules to create a safe working environment.	May use ground rules to create a safe working environment.
Family workers facilitate guided discovery and role play to promote understanding.	Supervisor may facilitate guided discovery and role-play to promote understanding.
Goal setting is central to the process.	Goal setting may be part of the process.
Homework tasks are assigned, to be completed between meetings.	Workers may be assigned tasks to be completed before the next session.
Family workers offer regular summaries to check their understanding.	Supervisor offers regular summaries to check his or her understanding.
Feedback is elicited from family members.	Feedback is elicited from the group.

In common with family meetings, it is useful to set ground rules for supervision sessions, agreed by all participants, in order to create a boundary for the group, within which it is possible to build rapport and trust. As the group members develop their working relationships, they may need to revisit these rules to reaffirm them or modify and/or discard any that no longer serve a useful purpose.

Only once trust has been established should the use of role-play be introduced in to supervision. As previously noted, it can then be very useful for exploring scenarios, developing skills and exploring all kinds of difficulties, as well as providing an opportunity to rehearse new skills in a comparatively safe environment. It can help family workers to practise working with their co-worker, and this provides an opportunity to generate ideas and problem solve in a situation that feels close to actual family work in practice. It may also offer the chance to explore the impossible or ridiculous: the 'I couldn't possibly say that' scenario. However, it may be best to avoid the use of role play if the group is not facilitated by someone skilled in its use, as it can be a very powerful medium, which can leave individuals with unresolved feelings if they are not helped at the end of the exercise to properly leave behind the role that they have played. Nonetheless, whether the group is facilitated or merely peer supervision among a group of new family workers, playing tapes is always a useful way to bring the reality of practice in to the session, to review progress and plan how to proceed.

Feedback is crucial to the purpose of supervision, but how this feedback is accepted (and therefore the learning derived from it) will depend on the quality of its delivery (Thompson 2005). To try to ensure that a supervisee's experience is as helpful as possible we suggest that those giving feedback apply the format shown in Box 7.4.

Box 7.4 Delivering effective feedback in supervision

Clear, explicit and specific
All feedback should clearly relate to an exact statement, behaviour or event, because if it is vague it may cause the supervisee anxiety and will therefore be less likely to improve his or her practice. The supervisee should be given information that helps him or her to do something with it, bearing in mind that it is hard to learn from generalised feedback.

Honest and owned
Feedback should be preceded by 'I find you...' rather than 'You are...', demonstrating that it is a personal opinion, not an irrefutable statement of truth. The feedback should include some justification, as without that it is unlikely to help the supervisee gain greater insight and is therefore meaningless.

Timely and regular
Feedback should be given as close to the event under discussion as possible, while it is still well remembered by all concerned. A supervisee should know when he or she could next expect to receive supervision, especially when trying out new skills. Knowing when the next session is scheduled to take place also helps a supervisee decide whether additional support needs to be sought following an unsettling experience in practice.

Prioritised
Most people cannot deal with more than three areas for improvement (Thompson 2005). It is therefore best to limit the number of items addressed in each session to three or fewer, leaving further issues to a later date when the initial priorities have been met.

Balanced and constructive
One of the main purposes of supervision is to open up possibilities for growth and development. This is unlikely to occur if the supervision sessions do not feel constructive. Therefore those giving feedback should always try to balance positive and negative comments. It is good practice to both start and finish with a positive statement, to try to ensure these are not overshadowed by a recipient's natural tendency to notice only the negative remarks.

It is useful to remember that supervision is a two-way process: within a supervisory relationship the behaviour and attitudes of the supervisee are just as important as those of the supervisor. Supervision is not a passive activity and we urge you to try to welcome any feedback as another's experience of you, listening carefully to what is being offered without reacting instantly. It is not necessarily about 'the truth', but what is said may have something useful for you within it, so we feel it is always worth taking time to reflect. Importantly, if you feel that the feedback is not precise or clear enough then you need to ask for this. The skills of supervisees can be examined further in the book *Supervision in the Helping Professions* (2006) by Hawkins and Shohet, and in our experience, having learned how to be a good supervisee, the skills and knowledge can be used to enable you to become an effective supervisor.

The practice issues brought to supervision and worked on within the session will be influenced by the interpersonal relationships that weave in and out of the process. Mental health workers (both supervisees and supervisors) inevitably have personal issues, including strengths and limitations, and from time to time supervision will need to focus on exploring the working relationships between group members and the group process itself (Hawkins and Shohet 2000), rather than the content of the interventions usually under discussion. Recognising this potential within the group's ground rules will facilitate the acknowledgement and resolution of any interpersonal conflict.

Just as preparation with your co-worker before a family meeting can help to give a boundary to your work and help you get a clearer sense of direction, the same is true for supervision. Discussing with your co-worker what you want to bring to the session, with some idea about what you hope to achieve or want from the group will enrich your experiences of supervision. Bringing notes for the other group members on the **demographic** features of the various family work participants, by using a **genogram**, as described in Chapter 8 (How to Conduct Family Work Assessments), will help focus the group on the details of your intervention. Then time will not be wasted within the session on material that can best be provided and assimilated through a written format.

Promoting awareness of family work for psychosis

Having worked out how to support its family workers, a mental health service provider is in a position to begin to try to offer family interventions in routine practice. As we described in Chapters 2 and 4, this needs to begin by promoting an awareness of what family work means in practice. This promotion may be achieved via a range of possibilities:

- presentations at conferences, mental health workers' team meetings, carers' groups, strategic mental health service providers' management fora, and so on

- informal word of mouth

- journal articles that either simply describe family work (for example, Leff 1998) or explore how it may be operationalised (for example, Smith and Velleman 2002)

- information leaflets, such as the one used in the Avon and Wiltshire Mental Health Partnership NHS Trust (AWP) that we have included as Appendix 4.

- websites such as www.familywork.org.uk and www.iris-initiative.org.uk.

Promotion of family work also results from the provision of the interventions in practice, through the energy and enthusiasm generated by its workers alongside service users and carers who recommend family work to others.

Generally in mental health services worldwide (and certainly within services throughout Britain) there are varying levels of family work provision, with some still debating whether or not they will provide family interventions. Others, such as AWP (DH 1999), have devoted resources to developing services over several years so that family work for psychosis is very widely available throughout their whole organisation. On the border between one mental health service provider's catchment area and anothers, carers and service users can get quite different information about family work and a range of responses to their requests for family intervention. It is recognised that such inequality is unacceptable so, for example, the government in Britain has tried to address these service discrepancies by producing best practice recommendations (NICE 2002). Workers elsewhere may find similar resources in their localities that try to promote equally good access to all for whom it may be appropriate, as described in Chapter 5 (When to Offer Family Work for Psychosis). Nevertheless, even with governmental support, achieving access to family interventions in everyday practice is not simple, although none of the barriers is insurmountable (Smith and Velleman 2002).

Referral

An effective referral process for family work for psychosis is described in Chapter 5, with a sample referral form given in Appendix 7, so within this chapter we will not discuss further how to generate appropriate family work referrals.

Having received a referral, family workers need to consider how best to engage the key family members, one of whom will always be the service user, as we know that he or she must be involved in at least some of the meetings for family interventions to be effective (Fadden 1998). Because the service user's involvement is vital we recommend that the first formal contact the family workers make with the family should be with the service user. The rationale for this is to try to ensure that the service user feels in control of the intervention and does not become swamped by the efforts of others trying to promote his or her recovery. In our experience, when the service user does experience a feeling of being overwhelmed, family work is quite likely to be refused by the service user, possibly because he or she is trying to achieve or maintain a sense of control that has been shown to reduce the distress associated with psychosis (Chadwick, Birchwood and Trower 1996).

In most cases it will only be once the service user has agreed to family work that the co-workers will arrange to meet other family members. This may be at a care planning meeting, such as a Care Programme Approach review (DH 1999), or a smaller get-together just between the family workers and carers, with or without the service user present.

There are occasions when the service user does not wish to be involved, as discussed in Chapter 4, but for the purposes of describing clearly how to proceed with our integrated model of family work we will presume the service user is a willing participant.

Initial meeting with family workers

A few families may be reluctant to even meet to consider the possibility of engaging in family interventions due to unpleasant past experiences of some aspect of mental health services. Sadly, their reasons often appear to include a traumatic experience of systemic family therapy. In such cases these former experiences need to be openly acknowledged during the family workers' early interactions with service users and carers; co-workers need to be prepared to hear these criticisms without feeling themselves to blame or becoming defensive, and without negating what the family is saying. Having aired any grievances it is then usually possible to discuss and clarify the purpose of family work, as described in Chapter 2, to help the family choose whether or not to engage.

There needs to be an overt acknowledgement that, even though the carers are being invited to engage with mental health services, there is no implication, as explained within Chapter 1 (Introduction), that the family is sick or perceived as sick. Moreover, the reason for suggesting their involvement (to help them to cope with the difficulties that have arisen from the service user's psychotic illness) may need to be reiterated several times to ensure that the purpose is well understood. This acknowledgement should include a strong statement from the family workers regarding their interest in exploring the family's strengths, as well as looking at areas of need. Families who have benefited from the intervention may themselves be willing to speak to service users and carers who are considering family work to possibly facilitate their engagement and reinforce the workers' assertions that it is a collaborative, non-judgemental approach.

This introductory meeting is also an opportunity for family members to tell the co-workers about some of their views on the cause and likely course of psychosis. Here we find it is useful to recall the Health Belief Model (HBM) proposed by Becker and Maiman (1975) that we described briefly in Chapter 2, so that a carer's or service user's comments can be considered under the following headings:

- perceived susceptibility or vulnerability
- perceived severity
- perceived benefits
- barriers to adherence or negative aspects of recommended behaviour.

The structure afforded by this model can help you to consider how the family may receive educational material. This is important because the information you proffer will not be assimilated if it does not fit in to the ways various family members have already begun to conceptualise the illness (Barrowclough and Tarrier 1997).

At the introductory meeting with family members it is usually best for the co-workers to avoid giving much specific detail about psychosis. This is because it is generally most useful to assess the service user's and carers' prior knowledge before imparting information, as without sufficient background it is very easy for workers to cause offence and/or distress, thus jeopardising the whole engagement process.

Introducing the concept of family work for psychosis

When meeting service users and carers for the first time we suggest that family workers do not introduce themselves as 'family workers', but try instead to explain something of their role by way of introduction. This is because using the title 'family worker' can lead to questions about what it means before the co-workers are in a position to judge the most appropriate way to explain it. For this reason, we find it useful to describe ourselves as mental health workers who work both with the service user and those providing him or her with help and support, in order to maximize that support, to reduce any unnecessary dependence on mental health services and to keep the need for statutory services' involvement to a minimum. We also declare our interest in helping to strengthen the resources of those who assist the service user to reduce the risk that their support collapses.

As explained in Chapter 2, it is useful for new family workers to practise introducing the concept of family work and differentiating it from systemic family therapy within supervision sessions or in the classroom if they are undertaking formal training. With their permission we have included in Box 7.5 some of the phrases devised by our students as they practised this skill. Not all the suggestions will be suitable for all families, but by combining elements from this list with the information you glean from colleagues who already know the family and that is included on the referral form, you are likely to be able to plan an appropriate introduction for a particular family.

To make the list most useful we have adopted the word 'psychosis' throughout Box 7.5; however, it is crucial that family workers never use this word without first checking the service user's and carers' position. Therefore it is vital in every case to begin by asking the family whether the service user's psychiatrist has given a diagnosis; if so this term should be used during the subsequent explanatory discussions. It is unwise for you and your co-worker to employ the terms schizophrenia, manic depression, bipolar disorder, psychosis or even serious mental illness if no diagnosis has been given to the family.

In practice you may find that you have contrary information from the service user's psychiatrist, who is clear about a diagnosis, yet the family asserts that none has been given. This would suggest to us that they have not heard the diagnosis and therefore may not be ready to accept it. In such cases, rather than repeat the diagnosis yourselves, we suggest that you report your findings back to the psychiatrist so that she or he can repeat the information. Your purpose as family workers can then include (as usual) helping the service user and carers make sense of what they have been told.

In situations where the family does not have or does not use a diagnostic term, the workers should gently explore the service user's and/or carers' explanatory framework and embrace this within their introduction of the concept of family work for psychosis.

Box 7.5 Introducing family interventions to service users and carers

- Thank you for agreeing to see us. We want to give you the chance to talk about X's psychosis and how you are managing now (including reference to specific reasons for referral from the referral form).

- What we are aiming for is to offer an opportunity for you to describe your experience of X's psychosis and talk about any stresses you are experiencing. Helping your family to understand how and why you might become distressed, may help you all cope if things get difficult.

- We believe the problems that you are experiencing at present may be due to X's psychosis, since any illness can cause families stress. We hope to join you in what you know already, offering the resources and experience we have gained through working with other families in situations similar to yours.

- We know that his or her family provide the majority of care for a service user who has psychosis and, over the years, will have developed ways of coping. Research has shown that family work can improve coping, understanding and problem solving, which can enhance relationships and reduce relapse rates.

- We are aware that you play the key role in supporting X. We are also aware that family work can help families in dealing more effectively with the consequences of psychosis. You may want to talk about the possibility of this work for your family and begin to think about your own needs.

- You may have specific requests for information – we will try to get you what you need, including information about how you can best help X, about X's psychosis or perhaps the side effects of medication.

- We aim to help you to solve problems in a way that will build on your strengths and allow you to become independent of our services. Problems may occur because of the effects of the psychosis on your daily activities. Our aim is to try to work together in finding out what helps and what doesn't help, and consider ways to try to accept what cannot change and deal with the consequences of that.

Further clarification about the style of family work and how it is delivered in practice may be offered through the following points.

- This work does not take the place of any other intervention; it is offered as an addition.

- Family workers visit regularly until it is agreed that the meetings have served their purpose.

- A structured approach is suggested to organise the time spent together in family meetings.

- Family workers will discuss how to deal with a crisis and help the family make a plan to be used should the need arise.

- Family workers will always try to meet at a time and in a place that suits everyone.

At times family workers will probably find themselves needing to remind other workers about the purpose of family interventions. In our experience, as workers become confident in their ability to explain family work for psychosis to service users and carers, the more able they are to discuss it with their colleagues and advocate on behalf of families in need.

Factors that decrease the likelihood that families will accept family work for psychosis

However competent your explanation of the concept of family work, there are a number of reasons, some of which are listed in Box 7.6, that make it less likely that a family will engage in family interventions.

Box 7.6 Factors that may reduce the likelihood of a family engaging in family intervention

Factors negatively affecting carers' and service users' engagement in family work include:

- the physical health and the age of carer; old and infirm carers are less likely to engage
- competing and unmanageable demands on the carer's emotional and/or material resources
- the carer's or service user's personal beliefs are incompatible with family work; this is particularly apparent if the service user has paranoid ideas that include the carer being part of a conspiracy to do him or her harm
- a lack of understanding about the illness
- a general feeling of apathy and pessimism within the family (sometimes known as burnout)
- residential instability
- the individual characteristics of either the carer or the service user
- dissatisfaction with a particular mental health practitioner and/or the treatment in general
- low or non-existent expectations that anything can make a difference or promote the service user's recovery.

Duration of the family work process
It is impossible to ascertain when first meeting a family how many meetings may take place. Nevertheless, it is vital to convey to the service user and carers that family intervention is a finite process, although you can assure them it will never end abruptly and that the ending will be negotiated by all concerned. It is usual to deliver this message at the introductory meeting.

Summary

We have tried to establish throughout this chapter the importance of preparing to undertake family work before accepting the referral of a family in need. This should include finding a co-worker, ensuring that both workers have a clear understanding of the whole family work process and setting up appropriate supervision arrangements. It is then practicable to accept a referral and meet all family members, beginning with the service user.

Practising the skill of introducing family work in a safe environment such as a classroom or supervision session increases the likelihood that workers will engage families in practice. A coordinated referral process which ensures that workers meet families within two to three weeks of the need for family work being identified also increases the likelihood that service users and carers will accept the intervention.

Using good supervision throughout the whole process of family intervention enables workers to be as effective as possible within the available resources. Limiting the workers' access to practice supervision is usually inefficient in the long run.

It is not the role of family workers to provide families with a medical diagnosis for the service user's condition. They can, however, do a great deal to help carers and service users to understand what a particular diagnostic term means and embrace this within their journey towards recovery.

Key points

- An awareness of family interventions can be achieved through a range of media, including leaflets, websites, journal articles and presentations.

- Testimonials from service users and carers who have benefited from family work can very effectively explain how family interventions work and encourage others to take part.

- When commencing family work, workers should keep in mind the whole conceptual process.

- Workers should have had some appropriate training and ensure they have access to adequate supervision before commencing family work in practice.

- A strongly developed working relationship between co-workers (well supported by practice supervision) will facilitate the provision of effective family interventions.

- New family workers should practise introducing the concept of family interventions within a classroom or supervision setting before attempting to explain it to a family in need.

- On receipt of a referral for family work, it is usual for one or both of the workers to meet the service user to engage him or her in the process before meeting other family members.

Recommended further reading

Department of Health (1999) *National Service Framework for Mental Health: Modern Standards and Service Models.* London: The Stationery Office.

Devane, S., Haddock, G., Lancashire, S., Baguley, I. *et al.* (1998) 'The Clinical Skills of Community Psychiatric Nurses Working with People who have Severe and Enduring Mental Health Problems: An Empirical Analysis.' *Journal of Advanced Nursing 27,* 253–260.

Hawkins, P. and Shohet, R. (2006) *Supervision in the Helping Professions* (3rd edn). Milton Keynes: Open University Press.

Kuipers, L., Leff, J. and Lam, D. (2002) *Family Work for Schizophrenia. A Practical Guide* (2nd edn). London: Gaskell.

Miklowitz, D. and Goldstein, M. (1997) *Bipolar Disorder. A Family-Focused Treatment Approach.* London: Guilford Press.

Miller, W. and Rollnick, S. (2002) *Motivational Interviewing. Preparing People to Change Addictive Behaviour* (2nd edn). London: Guilford Press.

Repper, J. and Perkins, R. (1996) *Working Alongside People with Long Term Mental Health Problems.* London: Chapman & Hall.

Sainsbury Centre for Mental Health (1998) *Keys to Engagement.* London: SCMH.

8

How to Conduct Family Work Assessments

The assessment process

There may be a temptation for family workers to 'get stuck in' and help families with the immediate difficulties they are facing. Indeed in some cases, as we have noted before, this may be necessary due to the pressing nature of the family's problems. Nonetheless, whenever possible it is worth one of the family workers spending time alone with each person who is hoping to take part in the family intervention, to gather their individual perspective by making use of a number of specific assessment tools identified on our family work flowchart (Figure 2.1) in Chapter 2 (What is Family Work for Psychosis?).

Prior to embarking on any of the assessments that pertain to family work, however, it is worth to taking a moment to reflect on why you might use a specific assessment tool. If we think about the word tool, using its usual dictionary definition – 'any device or implement used to carry out mechanical functions' (*Concise Oxford Dictionary* 1998, p.1468) – it reminds us that we need to know not only how to use the tool, but also when to use it and for what purpose. And so it is with our family work assessment tools; before beginning any assessment you need to ask yourself: 'What do I hope to achieve by using this assessment tool?'

In today's mental health services there is a vast array of assessments that mental health workers are expected to complete, and in our experience this can lead to a blind acceptance of them by workers who forget to consider why they are using each particular assessment tool. They may even do some assessments because everyone in their mental health team does them: a 'one size fits all' attitude. We do not wish to perpetuate this attitude, so will explain fully the purpose behind all our suggestions, in order that you and your co-worker can choose which ones to use to inform your purpose. By this we aim to ensure that you can defend your reasoning with service users, carers and/or colleagues if they are pressuring you to forego or cut short the assessment process.

For most family workers working within the Britain's health and social services, the Care Programme Approach (DH 1991a, 1991b) will be employed in all cases to organise and monitor the service user's mental health care. Elsewhere workers are likely to use similar care planning frameworks to fulfil a similar function, as dictated by local or national policies. Whatever system you use, it is likely that you will be familiar with the use of assessments as the first step in the care process, used to inform goal setting and thus the choice of intervention. These are followed by evaluation, further assessment, and so on, as care progresses.

Assessments can identify needs and/or problem areas and should also elicit current resources, strengths and coping strategies, although the latter three are sometimes forgotten, particularly (paradoxically) when the problems and needs appear overwhelming. Remembering to note the positives and the negatives as well as how we actually record and use the information that we gather will strongly reflect the philosophy that underpins our work. Collaborative approaches will be demonstrated by how information is shared, which can help to further develop our working relationships and build rapport with service users, carers and our colleagues.

The assessments that we use in family work are sometimes termed 'intervention assessments'. This means that the information we gain from the assessment will not only inform us about areas in which we can work with the family, to support positive outcomes such as a reduction in rates of relapse for the service user, but also through the time actually spent completing the assessment provide the carer or service user with some relief. This is noted particularly by carers who have undertaken the Relative Assessment Interview (Barrowclough and Tarrier 1997), as they commonly report the benefit they feel from having someone listen attentively to their story (Drage *et al.* 2004). We suggest therefore that to really gain the full potential from any assessment, we need to approach it with the same enthusiasm and interest that may drive us when engaged in more obviously helpful interventions, such as problem solving, as described in Chapter 10 (How to Promote Recovery Through Family Work), or helping the family cope with an immediate crisis.

So, when you use any of the assessment tools described within this chapter, we suggest that you ask yourself the following questions.

- What information do I feel I am lacking?
- Has this information already been gathered by another mental health worker?
- How much time can my co-worker and I devote to carrying out family work assessments?
- Will my proposed assessment tool elicit the information I need within the time available?
- Is there any other assessment tool that will more efficiently collect the information I am looking for?

Once your objectives are clear and you have considered how much time you can allocate to the assessments you will be better able to decide what tools are best suited to your purpose, within the context of the particular family with whom you are working. There may be cultural issues that you need to consider at this point, but because there are so many possibilities it is beyond the scope of this manual to offer specific guidance.

Family workers should aim to carry out the family work assessment interviews in a way that conveys their interest in the carers' and service user's well being. This can be difficult to achieve when using an unfamiliar assessment tool, so it may be useful for new workers to practise their use through role-play in the classroom, within supervision sessions and/or with their co-worker.

Assessment tools suggested on our family work process flowchart

Here we present a detailed explanation of the assessment tools for carers and service users included within our family work process flowchart (see Figure 2.1). We also mention alternatives that may be more useful in particular circumstances.

We do hope that, as you read this section, you will not be tempted to rush through the family work assessment process. In our experience it really is time well spent and does reduce the time needed in later stages of the intervention, because it means that you tend to be working from a knowledgeable, collaborative position.

The Relative Assessment Interview (Barrowclough and Tarrier 1997)

A global assessment is called for initially to gain the widest possible perspective of the relevant issues; in family work a **semi-structured interview** is most appropriate, giving a balance between direct questions and free-flowing conversation to elicit problems, strengths and needs. We favour the Relative Assessment Interview (RAI) because it embraces all the domains carers tend to want to discuss as well as including a final section for anything that the carer wishes to add that has not already been covered. A complete version of the RAI can be found in Barrowclough and Tarrier's book *Families of Schizophrenic Patients* (1997), in Appendix 1.

The aims of the RAI are listed in Box 8.1. To be most effective, it requires the family worker to be competent in using therapeutic communication skills, which include active listening such as reflection, paraphrasing and summarising, to develop a **therapeutic alliance** (Clarkson 1995) through which the carer is encouraged to share their experience of coping with the service user's psychosis. The RAI, as its name suggests, was designed for use with the relatives of the service user (whom we term carers), but it can easily be adapted for use with mental health workers or a service user.

Box 8.1 Aims of the Relative Assessment Interview

In a conversational style the Relative Assessment Interview aims to:

- gather detail about the composition of the household, how family members spend their time and how much time individuals spend together

- obtain details of the service user's mental health history, including hospital admissions and treatments prescribed, as well as his or her symptoms, behaviours and social functioning (including past and/or current interests and activities)

- elicit the carer's responses to the service user and the psychosis, covering their behaviours, beliefs, thoughts and feelings

- find out about the carer's resources, including any positive and successful coping responses employed by the family, as well as areas of difficulty and non-coping, which may include irritability and/or violent outbursts.

When working with a family coping with an acute first episode of psychosis you may decide the RAI has too much focus on past events. In such cases the global assessment described by Addington and Burnett (2004) is likely to be more relevant, usefully taking the place of the Knowledge About Schizophrenia Interview (Barrowclough *et al.* 1987) too. However, in such cases family workers need to ensure they allocate time flexibly to carry out this assessment as the early stages of psychosis can be bewildering and generate strong emotions. It is unhelpful to encourage a carer to begin to explore his or her feelings and then stop the conversation at an inappropriate point because you have run out of time, leaving the carer to manage the distress alone.

Having undertaken a broad assessment, more specific tools can be employed to identify areas of particular concern and gain a deeper understanding of them. We strongly recommend the assessments that follow for their workability, the quality and clarity of the information elicited, and their apparent **validity** and **reliability**.

The Family Questionnaire (Barrowclough and Tarrier 1997)

The Family Questionnaire (FQ) contains a checklist of possible service user-focused problems and provides three five-point scales on which they can be rated. The first rating measures how often a particular behaviour or difficulty occurs, the second measures the amount of distress this causes, while the third gauges the carer's level of coping with that particular difficulty. (In fact, this third scale includes the word 'control' as well as 'cope' (Barrowclough and Tarrier 1997, p.196), but these two may not always occur together. Having discussed this with Professor Tarrier, we now recommend that you rate only coping.)

There is a later version of the FQ, which rates concerns, distress and coping on a three-point scale rather than the original five. This means that a score of 1 has come to depict 'never' and 'rarely' instead of just 'never' as it did in the five-point rating. We find this confusing as a rare occurrence such as a violent incident can be very hard to cope with and/or cause a great deal of distress; we therefore continue to use the original version.

The information gathered is then used to determine the main areas of concern to be addressed through further intervention. The FQ will also identify any strengths or coping strategies, which can then be developed and generalised to help the carer cope more effectively in those areas currently causing distress. It may be repeated at intervals to monitor progress and evaluate outcomes. A compete version of the FQ can be found in Barrowclough and Tarrier's book *Families of Schizophrenic Patients* (1997), in Appendix 2.

While this assessment tool can provide family workers with extremely informative details from carers about the difficulties they are facing with regard to the service user's psychosis, it is worth noting that this specificity can at times cause a problem. This may either be in terms of distress to the carer as they come to recognise the magnitude of what they are coping with, or distress to the service user as he or she becomes aware of the carer's responses. It can be useful therefore to forewarn family members that the reality they face when completing this assessment may be upsetting, to enable them to brace themselves. It is also useful to explain to them how this detail can really help to focus the family work and thereby increase its effectiveness, which may encourage them in its use.

The General Health Questionnaire (28) (Goldberg and Williams 1988)

The General Health Questionnaire (28) (GHQ) offers a means to assess the well-being of carers because it is designed for use with the general population, not those already diagnosed with a mental health problem, so is appropriately **sensitive**. The questions are presented in the form of four discrete checklists on which the carer rates her/his current situation compared to what they would consider to be their usual state, to judge the impact of their caring roles and responsibilities. An obvious drawback with this questionnaire is that if a problem has existed for some time, and due to its chronicity is perceived as 'usual', it will not therefore be scored as a problem. The worker needs to be aware of this possibility when a carer's response to the GHQ registers no problems or a low score that is out of keeping with the carer's appearance. Thus it may be that, where problems have existed for an extended period, the Symptom Rating Scale (Kellner and Sheffield 1973), which rates the presence of psychological distress in terms of 'often', 'sometimes' and 'never' regardless of when they started, will be more informative.

The GHQ (or Symptom Rating Scale) can be repeated to monitor progress and as an outcome measure for family work. However, in our experience carers are often reluctant to complete questionnaires that relate directly to themselves (rather than their responses to the service user as is usually the case with most family work assessments). We therefore advise family workers to be wary of basing the judgement of the success of their family interventions on the results of these scores alone. Nonetheless, they may be used to confirm, or otherwise, data from **qualitative** sources.

The four sub-scales of the GHQ (28), as shown in Box 8.2, each contain seven questions. The response to each of these questions is rated with a score of zero if there is not a problem or if it is no worse than usual; a score of one is given if the problem is worse or much worse than usual. The scores are then aggregated, with the maximum possible being 28. A score between zero and four indicates no mental health problems, a score between five and eleven denotes cause for concern and above 12 suggests the need for a referral for further help. A high score in just one sub-scale (although this could not reach the threshold of 12)

Box 8.2 Dimensions of psychological distress measured by the GHQ (28)

The General Health Questionnaire (28) encompasses the following four dimensions:

1. somatic symptoms

2. anxiety symptoms

3. social functioning

4. symptoms of depression.

could suggest that treatment is still indicated and would need to be discussed further with the carer concerned.

It may be that family work will be sufficient to resolve the carer's distress and improve the situation without the need for any other intervention, but in some cases a carer may need to seek treatment for their own mental health problem, before focusing on family interventions.

Although we recommend this assessment (and have permission to use it for training purposes on Thorn programmes), we must draw your attention to the fact that it is not currently in the public domain, so services need to purchase it from its publisher if they wish to use it in practice. It may be most appropriate to discuss the use of this tool within your organisation's practice governance forum rather than your team manager, as it may need to be a corporate decision to purchase it and recommend its use.

The Knowledge About Schizophrenia Interview (Barrowclough *et al.* 1987)

The Knowledge About Schizophrenia Interview (KASI) is designed with open and closed questions, as well as further prompts to estimate the carer's behaviour, attitudes and level of knowledge with regard to schizophrenia in general, and the specific nature of the illness as it affects their relative. It explores a range of issues under the six headings listed in Box 8.3, to give the family workers a detailed picture of the carer's understanding, plus pointing to areas where some education may be beneficial. A complete version of the KASI and how to score it can be

---

Box 8.3 The domains covered by the Knowledge About Schizophrenia Interview

The Knowledge About Schizophrenia Interview is divided into the following sections:

- diagnosis
- symptoms
- aetiology
- medication
- prognosis
- management.

found in Barrowclough and Tarrier's book *Families of Schizophrenic Patients* (1997), in Appendix 5.

Although the KASI was obviously designed to be specific to the diagnosis of schizophrenia, we have evolved its use and found it to be a helpful measure with regard to psychosis in general. Indeed, the questions do not need to be changed and it can be modified by simply replacing the word schizophrenia with psychosis in the title. In practice, this adaptation has a number of advantages:

- a relative finding it hard to accept the service user's diagnosis of schizophrenia may feel more able to complete the assessment
- it allows the usefulness of the assessment to be extended beyond the confines of one discrete diagnostic group
- sometimes, even when a psychiatrist has diagnosed schizophrenia, a carer may not have absorbed this information; in such cases it is often distressing to see the word schizophrenia on an assessment
- it can be used if the diagnosis is unclear, particularly in early intervention.

It must be remembered that adapting an assessment tool changes its validity and could impact on the reliability of its scoring. However, in routine practice (when not conducting research), the scores are less important than the detail elicited through the questions, so nowadays we find ourselves more often using the Knowledge About Psychosis Interview (KAPI), rather than the KASI from which it is derived.

The KASI or KAPI usually take between 10 and 30 minutes to complete, depending on how much the carer wishes to elaborate and in some cases can be incorporated into an RAI. If a carer seems to want to discuss their views about psychosis at greater length it is generally best to encourage him or her to wait until the family gets together in family meetings, so that everyone can benefit from each other's knowledge and opinions. The exception to this would be if the interview provokes a carer's grief, in which case it is often more helpful to spend time alone with him or her to explore these feelings. This may need to occur before commencing family meetings, or continue concurrently, depending on the impact of these feelings.

As with the RAI it is important to use a conversational approach when conducting the KASI and to be sure not to convey any impression that it is a test with right or wrong answers. Rather, it marks the first steps towards building your working relationship with the carer.

The way to score the KASI can initially appear complicated and may need some clarification to ensure that family workers feel able to apply a score to the interview if they wish. However, the use of the KASI is not dependent on its scoring, as in practice it is the detail included within the answers that is of most interest to us as family workers, rather than the score we assign. Nevertheless, scoring can be valuable if gaining knowledge about schizophrenia is to be used as an outcome measure in research or service development.

Scoring the KASI adheres to some general principles throughout.

- Each of the six sections is scored on a four-point scale, 1 to 4.

- A score of 1 generally means an 'incorrect' or unhelpful answer, possibly even shows attitudes or incorrect knowledge that could be damaging to the service user.

- A score of 2 demonstrates a lack of knowledge that can generally be corrected through education, but with no evidence of malevolent intent.

- A score of 3 generally means a 'correct' or a useful answer.

- A score of 4 demonstrates a very high level of knowledge.

- A score of less than 3 will guide you, as you and your co-worker consider the level and amount of educative intervention required to meet the family's needs.

Each section has specific scoring criteria and explanations for every question asked, which we suggest you critically consider before actually using the assessment tool, as some of the responses deemed to be 'correct' (Barrowclough *et al.* 1987, p.223) may not marry up with your own philosophical view about psychosis. We urge you to discuss any difficulties you have with the content or use of this assessment in the classroom or supervision, before attempting to carry it out in practice. From your discussions you may feel that scoring the KASI requires that the worker scoring has some ability to make a clinical judgement and it is worth noting that it was devised for use by a number of very skilled mental health practitioners. Nevertheless, in our experience, family workers, following a short training session, are easily able to achieve **inter-rater reliability** when scoring the KASI.

Service user global assessment

You will notice that there is no global assessment recommended on the service user side of our family work process flowchart (shown in Figure 2.1). This is a purposeful omission, because we feel it is beyond the scope of a family worker to complete such an assessment, unless they are the care coordinator and/or providing individual therapy too.

In practice, when in receipt of any psychosocial intervention, it is usually important for the service user to complete a global assessment, such as the

Manchester Scale or KGV as it is frequently known (Krawiecka, Goldberg and Vaughn 1977, modified by Lancashire 1998) or the Brief Psychiatric Rating Scale (Overall and Gorham 1962), to gain some **phenomenological** understanding of his or her mental health problems. It is not necessary for family workers to conduct this assessment, but for family work to be really effective it is vital that the service user is prepared to share some of the outcomes of this assessment with the family workers to inform the education process, and so on.

As you will see from our explanation of the family work education process, described in Chapter 9 (How to Manage a Successful Family Work Meeting) we hope to promote the service user as 'the expert' (Falloon *et al.* 1984, p.140). By this we aim to help him or her to acknowledge having had a personal experience of psychosis, using that position to inform others within the safe structure of family work meetings. Moreover, it often helps the service user to rehearse this sharing with one of the family workers before discussing it with family members. Therefore before the education-focused family meetings commence this family worker should arrange to spend time with the service user to develop a clear understanding of what will be shared. Within these individual sessions some other more specific assessments also may be carried out to give a more detailed understanding of medication-related issues and the service user's social functioning.

It is likely that the worker carrying out this planning and the individual assessments will develop an alliance with the service user that will continue into the family meetings; this can work well and provide strong support to the service user, as well as protection (if necessary) from intrusive questioning from other family members keenly trying to enhance their knowledge and understanding of psychosis. However, if the workers feel it is important for the service user to build a relationship equally with both of them, they may each carry out one or two of the following assessments.

Social Functioning Scale (Birchwood *et al.* 1990)

The Social Functioning Scale (SFS) is designed to assess the social functioning of individuals with a diagnosis of schizophrenia; the scoring therefore relates to this population. It assesses a number of areas of functioning in social situations, as listed in Box 8.4, which may need to be targeted and addressed through family interventions. It also captures and celebrates areas of ability and/or strength that can be built upon either within individual therapy or family work.

The SFS assesses behaviours associated with social engagement and/or withdrawal. It then assesses whether the competences possessed by the service user are actually put into practice. The score of this self-report by the service user of his or her social functioning is compared to the scores of others with a similar diagnosis,

Box 8.4 Domains covered by the Social Functioning Scale

The areas of the service user's social functioning covered by the SFS are:

- social engagement and/or withdrawal
- interpersonal functioning, including number of friends, and the quality of relationships and communication
- social and recreational activities
- independence, in terms of possessing the competence to perform the skills listed
- independence, in terms of actually performing the skills listed
- employment/occupation/structured therapeutic programme carried out on a daily basis.

which is considered to be more relevant than comparing service user to the general population, who may not have had their career and personal developments interrupted by psychosis. Nonetheless, we urge you to refer to the Early Psychosis Declaration (WHO 2004) when carrying out the SFS, to remind yourself that a loss of functioning (and a loss of expectations) is not an inevitable outcome of psychosis, to avoid falling into the trap of therapeutic pessimism.

We find the SFS is actually a very useful assessment tool within family work, as it is able to offer a lot of precise information, usually within a relatively short space of time and in a way that service users appear willing to accept. Moreover, the elicited issues relating to social functioning often seem to be one of the main sources of stress and distress within a family referred for family interventions. Its format allows the service user to record his or her own social and recreational activities that have not been specifically asked about and, in our experience of using the SFS over a number of years, it has become increasingly necessary for service users to add new activities to represent ways that young people in the twenty-first century are likely to behave (whether or not they are diagnosed with schizophrenia). This flexibility keeps the SFS up to date and avoids the need to devise and validate a new tool.

If repeated at intervals (either within family work or individual therapy) the SFS can usefully act as a means to monitor progress or as an outcome measure at the end of intervention. A complete version of this assessment tool can be found in Barrowclough and Tarrier's book *Families of Schizophrenic Patients* (1997), in Appendix 3.

The Manchester Short Assessment of Quality of Life Scale (Priebe *et al.* 1999)

The Manchester Short Assessment of Quality of Life Scale (MANSA) provides a structure for an interview by which to assess quality of life in a way that reflects the philosophy underpinning psychosocial interventions, through a measure of recovery from mental illness that is not simply captured in terms that relate to symptom reduction. It covers a broad range of issues, requiring that the service user judge his or her own situation, rather than these judgements being made by mental health workers or carers. While it frequently takes only a few minutes to complete, it can lead to a deeper understanding of the service user's experience beyond that of symptoms of illness, as well as trying to quantify the felt satisfaction with his or her life.

The MANSA is relatively easy to use, although in our experience the questions relating to crime and physical violence seem to interrupt the flow. It is sensitive to changes in the service user's situation and ensures that the important issue of quality of life is on the agenda of all concerned with his or her mental health care. The assessment is structured in three sections, as shown in Box 8.5.

Box 8.5 Components of the MANSA Quality of Life Scale

The MANSA is divided into three parts as follows.

- *Section 1* documents personal details – for example, name and date of birth – so needs to be completed only once.

- *Section 2* relates to circumstances that may change from time to time, such as the service user's address and employment details.

- *Section 3* comprises 16 subjective questions that are rated using a **Likert scale** to quantify the service user's responses in relation to his or her satisfaction with life within a number of areas, including financial situation, relationship with others, sex life, leisure activities, personal safety, accommodation and living alone, if appropriate. It also has four objective questions requiring a 'yes' or 'no' answer, which relate to having friends, the number of contacts with others per week, any involvement in crime and experience of physical violence.

It is important to note that many of the questions included in the MANSA interview schedule relate to very personal information, which service users might be reluctant to disclose. For this reason this tool should be used only within the context of a therapeutic relationship, with clarification established about how the information will be used and with whom it will be shared.

Drug Attitude Inventory (Hogan *et al.* 1983)

The version of the Drug Attitude Inventory (DAI) that we prefer comprises 30 items; there is a version with only 10 items, but in practice we have found it less satisfactory than the longer one. To complete the DAI a service user reads each statement and then records whether he or she either agrees or disagrees with it. The inventory identifies beliefs about the effects of medication (both positive and negative), the long-term goals related to using medication (or not), the need for medication, and the control and/or choices involved in medication use.

The DAI can be repeated over time, and is especially useful when a change of medication is being considered. It may be most helpful to inform a plan to change over depot injections to oral medication, eliciting the service user's attitudes and beliefs as a predictor of compliance with the new regimen.

While the DAI provides a means to broadly quantify a service user's views, in order to explore the likelihood that he or she will take medication, answers to individual items can also be very significant. For example, a service user may initially be willing to take lithium, but may well believe their medication is poisonous – a concern that would be elicited by one of the DAI statements. Knowledge of this concern enables the prescriber to address it, which in the case of lithium would include explaining the signs of toxicity and the purpose of regular blood tests, thus allaying any unfounded fears and increasing the likelihood that medication is used to best effect.

Despite the known effectiveness of **neuroleptic medication** (Kane 1989) its use may not be viewed in a positive manner by a service user, which in turn affects the likelihood that he or she will take it. Given that neuroleptic medication can both reduce the experience of psychotic symptoms and lessen the risk of relapse it is useful to have a means to discuss and try to understand the service user's beliefs relating to medication use. The DAI provides a validated framework within which to have this discussion.

As the DAI predicts concordance with medication by examining an individual's attitudes and beliefs, it is likely to be more acceptable to service users than techniques (such as a pill count) that gather hard evidence of compliance. Nonetheless, it needs to be administered in the context of a therapeutic working relationship and supplemented with further questions to be fully informative and useful. The detailed conversations generated by a service user's responses to the DAI can start to identify previous negative experiences of treatment that have not been aired before, which will inform the overall process of medication management (Gray 2002).

The scoring of the DAI compares service user's perceptions of medication with the 'ideal' answers that are deemed to correspond to fully compliant attitudes and beliefs about medication. If the service user's response is not 'ideal' it is given a negative score, while those that are 'ideal' are given a positive one. The total score is achieved by subtracting the number of negative responses from the number of positive ones. At the extremes this could be minus 30 from plus zero (giving a final total of minus 30), or minus zero from plus 30 (giving a final total score of plus 30). The total then provides a measure of compliance with medication, with a positive score denoting the likelihood of concordance, a negative score the risk of non-compliance. There is the possibility of a maximum score of 30 and the closer the score is to this number, the greater the service user's conviction in whichever direction is suggested by the positive or negative prefix.

The Liverpool University Neuroleptic Side Effect Rating Scale (Day *et al.* 1995)

The Liverpool University Neuroleptic Side Effect Rating Scale (LUNSERS) is a self-rating scale that can be quick and easy to use. (It may be conducted as an interview, but the validity of the scores relates to its use as a self-rated tool.) It acknowledges a range of potential side effects that neuroleptic medication may induce, assesses whether they are actually present and, if so, to what extent. This in turn allows the side effects to be addressed and may encourage greater concordance with the prescribed medication regimen.

The LUNSERS comprises 51 items, divided into the categories listed in Box 8.6. Forty-one items are genuine potential side effects of neuroleptic medication, with the remaining ten called 'red herrings' (Day *et al.* 1995, p.650), included as a means to identify service users who tend to assign a high score to everything or those completing the scale inaccurately.

To complete the LUNSERS, service users are asked to rate all 51 questions as follows.

- To each item assign a rating between from zero to 4 depending on how frequently the side effect has occurred over the past month.

- Zero equates to 'not at all', 1 represents 'very little', 2 means 'a little', 3 means 'quite a lot' and 4 equates to 'very much'.

- An additional column has been added to rate the distress felt as a result of the side effect. This is scored out of 10, with a score of 3 interpreted as 'not very distressing' and 7 or above said to be 'very distressing'.

Box 8.6 Categories in the Liverpool University Neuroleptic Side Effect Rating Scale

The LUNSERS organises the potential side effects associated with the use of neuroleptic medication into the following categories:

- anticholinergic symptoms, such as difficulty in passing water
- extra-pyramidal symptoms, such as shakiness
- hormonal symptoms, such as a swollen or tender chest
- other autonomic symptoms, such as dizziness
- allergic reactions, such as itchy skin
- psychic side effects, such as increased dreaming
- miscellaneous symptoms, such as pins and needles.

There is an eighth category of symptoms not expected as side effects of neuroleptic medication (known as red herrings) that act as a control.

A final score of 20 or above indicates significant side effects in terms of their frequency and suggests that medication should be reviewed. Therefore the LUNSERS is of value to service users taking neuroleptic medication, providing an objective means to rate the occurrence and severity of side effects, and prompting their inclusion on the agenda of care planning meetings. It is particularly useful because it assesses such a wide range of potential side effects (including the hormonal symptoms that so often seem to get ignored, possibly because they can be embarrassing to discuss) and the distress they cause, which can all have an impact on a service user's willingness to accept medication. It should be noted that a side effect that occurs rarely may be no less distressing (and, for instance, an **oculogyric crisis** can be more so) than one that is present all the time. The level of distress is therefore potentially very influential to the service user's choice regarding whether or not to use medication.

There are some questions within the LUNSERS that relate to sexual function; these are most appropriately discussed within an individual therapeutic working relationship and not in a family meeting. Even so, the gender of the worker may need to be considered in order to help the service user to discuss particularly sensitive or potentially embarrassing issues.

The inclusion of the red herrings needs to be explained to the service user. They are included to provide an opportunity to clarify the possible cause of the experiences identified; they are in no way meant to catch the service user out. When scoring the LUNSERS it is necessary to be mindful that the service user is as susceptible to minor ailments as anyone else, so a positive response to one of the red herrings could relate to a physical illness. For example, reporting a runny nose (which is one of the red herring questions) could be due to having a common cold, but as far as completing the LUNSERS according to its instructions, is correctly recorded as it has been present within the previous month. This reminds us that all responses should be acknowledged and explored.

If side effects are identified it is then possible to consider ways to manage them, allowing medication to be used with the minimum disruption to the service user's normal functioning. It can therefore be helpful to quantify the experience of side effects and put them in priority order for either problem solving in family meetings, or discussion with the care coordinator or the doctor prescribing the neuroleptic medication. Categorising the side effects can help link them to the profile of the prescribed neuroleptic medication, which can help to guide the doctor when choosing a possible alternative. For example, if the extra-pyramidal side effects of one of the older neuroleptics are causing problems, switching to an **atypical antipsychotic medication**, rather than another **typical antipsychotic medication** (with the probability it will have a similar side effect profile) would be likely to be most successful.

There is an obvious need for the doctor prescribing the service user's neuroleptic medication to be aware of the LUNSERS, since its use is quite likely to prompt some kind of medication review, or at least more informed questioning of the doctor by the service user. And even if the prescription is not altered radically, the time of taking the neuroleptic medication or the way the dosage is divided may be changed, to improve the service user's experience.

However, prior to any change in the ways the neuroleptic medication is used, a mental health assessment such as the KGV (Krawiecka *et al.* 1977, modified by Lancashire 1998) is recommended to give a baseline measure of troublesome symptoms against which to consider any progress over time. Nonetheless, as mentioned previously, this time-consuming assessment is beyond the resources of most family workers, so needs to be considered by the care coordinator, who is in a position to decide how it may be carried out. This demonstrates an example of why family interventions must be integrated into the service user's overall care plan, as without this integration family workers can be left recommending interventions that no one carries out, which is obviously frustrating for all concerned.

It is important to recognise that a change of prescription is not the only means to manage the side effects of neuroleptic medication. For example, some service users may opt to experiment with alternatives such as a change of dietary intake and/or an increase in activity levels to manage a gain in their weight rather than change the prescription if they feel it is suiting them in terms of managing their symptoms of psychosis. Planning and support through family meetings can be key to the success of such strategies.

The LUNSERS, as its name implies, is not designed to detect side effects of medication such as lithium, antidepressants or drugs used for physical conditions. However, its results must be viewed in the light of any medications in addition to the neuroleptics that the service user may be taking. Thus, it is vital to note down all substances used (both prescribed and non-prescribed) and consider their impact before any side effects can be attributed solely to neuroleptic medication. These other substances may include prescriptions for opiate dependence and/or illicit substances, so this needs to be explored sensitively and may necessitate a search for information about how various drugs interact and their known effects and side effects.

The LUNSERS can, then, generate a wealth of information and prompt wide-ranging discussions. Each response can be viewed as a qualitative comment on the current experience, within a structure that allows for a conversation about issues pertinent to the service user and his or her treatment. As the service user creates a hierarchy of areas to be worked on, setting targets for change within a framework of care provided by a whole team of mental health workers, you may as family workers need to be especially careful that the agenda you are working on is the same as others'. For example, it is not uncommon for a rare but very distressing side effect to be singled out for attention in family meetings where family members are in touch with each other's distress, while other mental health workers prioritise the frequently occurring side effects that are more noticeable. It is usually advisable that only one problem is tackled at a time so that the effectiveness of possible solutions can be judged properly. Clear communication and care planning between all concerned is therefore essential, ideally with the service user orchestrating the whole process.

Summary

After the initial introductory meeting (or meetings) there are a number of assessment tools that can be used with the service user and/or carers to determine what intervention may be most useful, as well as the various family members' strengths that may form the basis for developing new coping strategies.

Key points

- Family work assessments, through their non-judgemental approach and conversational style, can serve as a therapeutic intervention in their own right.

- Each assessment should be chosen carefully to try to ensure that it is the best tool to elicit the details required.

- Service users and carers report that family work assessments are in themselves therapeutic as well as useful in informing future interventions.

Recommended further reading

Barrowclough, C. and Tarrier, N. (1997) *Families of Schizophrenic Patients.* Cheltenham: Stanley Thornes.

Gray, R. (2002) 'Medication Management for People with a Diagnosis of Schizophrenia.' *Nursing Times 98*, 47, 38–40.

Smith, J. (2000) *Early Warning Signs. A Self Management Training Manual for Individuals with Psychosis.* Worcestershire Community and Mental Health Trust.

Recommended web-based resources

www.nmhct.nhs.uk/Pharmacy/ – This site is provided by the pharmacy service within Norfolk and Waveney Mental Health Partnership NHS Trust and supported on the Trust server. It receives no hidden commercial backing or bias, and was the first UK multi-page hospital pharmacy website. Visit it find out more about drug treatments that are prescribed for mental health needs.

9

How to Manage a Successful Family Work Meeting

Bringing a family together and sharing information from the individual assessments

When you and your co-worker have completed all your chosen assessments with each family member you will be ready to arrange the first family work meeting. The main purpose of this meeting is to begin to share the information given by the service user and carers, during their individual assessments with either one of the family workers, that they have agreed they want other family members to know. You will have already made it clear to all members of the family that anything they say to one worker is shared with the other worker within your co-working arrangement. In our experience it is useful to have a framework to contain the shared material, so we created a document that we merely call the Family Work Assessment (FWA) form to fulfil this function. We have included it here as Appendix 9.

We intend that the FWA form is taken to this first family work meeting and that workers (as long as there are no other more pressing agenda items) introduce its structure and intended purpose to those present. We find it is usually possible within this first meeting to also introduce the rationale for having some ground rules that will help to facilitate the smooth running, and thereby the effectiveness, of future family meetings.

It is quite likely that the service user and carers will not have items for the family work meeting's agenda at this early stage, because they are still not absolutely sure how to use the process. Nonetheless, from the outset family workers should begin meetings (after a quick catch-up on how things have been since the last get-together) by setting an agenda, agreeing how to prioritise the items and allocating time to each one. So discussing the structure for recording information and setting ground rules provides a useful demonstration of how to use the meetings, including (as will be evident from the prepared material brought by the workers) the value of considering in advance what to discuss. Equally, as we have stated earlier in this manual, the family you are working with may be struggling with an immediate issue. In this situation you will have to decide with the family whether this struggle must take priority, and in some cases it is right that it should. However, you may find the family is repeatedly bringing new crises to every family meeting, thus denying you the opportunity to introduce new ways of working together; if so you may need to discuss it in supervision to plan a way forward.

In practice, a useful way to differentiate a family's genuine need for help to deal with immediate crises, as opposed to a family that presents you with a series of problems that obstruct the development of new strategies, is to ask yourselves as family workers how these crises appear to you. Our rule of thumb is this: if the family seems to be dealing with 'one thing after another', which means that their crises are all somewhat different, then we would judge these crises as appropriate for our immediate intervention. However, if it appears that the family is struggling with 'the same old thing', meaning that the current crisis is the same as others they have asked you to help with before, we suggest you point this out in a non-critical way. It may be useful to do this alongside a suggestion that if family members learn more about each other (including their strengths) and try to develop new ways of coping, they are more likely to be able to deal with their crises themselves, rather than remaining dependent on others. To help to ensure that those asking for help do not feel unheard and that their concerns are not forgotten, it may be useful at this stage to begin to make a list of problems to be addressed at a later date when a problem-solving structure has been learned. If one particular family member keeps presenting you with problems, it can be effective to ask that person to be responsible for maintaining an up-to-date list of these problems and concerns. This list can then be reviewed at the beginning of each family meeting to check whether anything on it is of greater priority than any other planned agenda items.

Setting ground rules

While not all families have difficulty in communicating clearly with each other, in some families there are patterns of communication that are not helpful when trying to cope with psychosis. Particular barriers to effective discussion include when family members do not take turns in speaking but instead tend to interrupt each other when wishing to say something, or when one person dominates all conversations. Nevertheless, in practice we find that most families coping with psychosis (whether or not they have previously been very skilled communicators) benefit from some help. This is likely to include evolving some ground rules for how to behave during family meetings to ensure that everyone has an opportunity to speak and everybody's contributions are still heard if these meetings become emotionally charged.

We need to be sure that our suggestions proffered to help promote clear communication between family members do not in themselves communicate an implied criticism of the family's current skills and/or attempts to cope with psychosis. We have found it useful therefore to explain to a family that, at points of heightened anxiety or during intense conversations when everyone has something to say, the worker facilitating the family meeting may need some ground rules to draw on so that everyone present can hear others' contributions. These rules will be particular to each family that you work with, negotiated at the start of your regular meetings together and possibly reiterated during subsequent meetings as required. To give you some ideas for what may be included, we have listed in Box 9.1 some suggested ground rules that are likely to facilitate effective family work.

Box 9.1 Suggested ground rules to promote effective family meetings

Ground rules to facilitate effective family meetings may include the following.

- Only one person speaks at any one time.
- Everyone is offered an equal opportunity to speak during each family meeting.
- People will address each other directly and avoid speaking about another in the third person.
- Everyone has the right to leave a family meeting at any point, for as long as necessary. Should this happen, it is usual that the individual is invited to return as soon as possible, but whether or not he or she returns on this occasion does not affect the invitation to the next meeting. Decisions may also need to be reached in advance about whether or not the business of the meeting should continue while any individual is absent and whether an individual who leaves a meeting should be followed, to offer them comfort and/or help them to return.
- Respect will be shown for each other's feelings at all times throughout family meetings.
- All suggestions made will be offered and accepted in the spirit of cooperation to promote coping and recovery.

Where physical or verbal aggression has been a feature of a family's interactions (whether this was in the past or is ongoing) this should be acknowledged, with appropriate ground rules put in place to ensure that everyone present (including the workers) feels safe during all family work meetings.

You might also consider including a ground rule that relates to your co-working arrangements, to help you decide whether or not to meet if one of the workers is unexpectedly unable to attend. It is our suggestion that you do include such a ground rule and that you generally agree to cancel a meeting if it is not possible for both workers to be there. You may include a proviso that a single worker would meet in an emergency to help the family find a solution to an immediate problem, but you would not cover any new skills development in the absence of a co-worker.

Communication skills

It is not a feature of any of our family work meetings to develop specific communication skills using role-play, as advocated by Falloon and colleagues (1984). As other effective family work models (for example, Kuipers *et al.* 2002) have not included it we presume it is not essential to the delivery of evidence-based family interventions. Nevertheless, we recognise the value of clear communication that promotes positive encouragement and limits negative comments whenever possible. Therefore within our family work any difficulties in communication are noted by the workers from the first family get-together and addressed during this or subsequent family meetings as they arise, at a time when the workers judge that the service user and/or carers are likely to be most receptive to the suggested alternatives. This is usually achieved through modelling by the family workers, although there may be some occasions when family members will be encouraged to role-play a particular new skill within a meeting to get an instant response to it.

Understanding boundaries and avoiding resistance

A broad aim of our family work is to help reduce the stress that results from the service user's psychosis as experienced by various family members. In addition to promoting clear communication as a means to reduce the tension within family relationships we are also concerned with what we term 'the boundaries' between individuals within the family, and the boundaries the whole family places between itself and the outside world. This necessitates family workers being clear about any information they give to the service user and/or carers as well as that they receive, noting how information is communicated between family members and adhering initially to what they observe to be the rules within the **family system**. This adherence demonstrates a wish to **join** the family and thereby facilitates discussions about how the family members are currently coping and the difficulties they face so that you can begin to try to help individuals and the whole family to clarify these rules and the roles individuals adopt. The way that you communicate with each other is an opportunity to model clear boundaries, rather than the rigid or diffuse ones (as explained later in this section) that often emerge in response to trying to manage or limit the impact of various tensions. Over time it is then usually possible to discuss during family meetings the value that having clear boundaries can bring.

If we look at a family as a system, we can observe a structure (that involves close family members, more distant relatives and any number of significant others), a communication system (that relates to how instructions, events and feelings are shared or not), and allocated or adopted roles (concerning who does what, and when and how they do it) within that system (Wright 1989). Their family is usually the first system that an individual is a part of, and only later will he or she join other systems, such as school, clubs, employment, and so on. Every family has a **belief system** that contains the attitudes, ideas and opinions that the family as a whole believe to be true; this belief system strongly influences the behaviour of the various family members towards each other, through what are known as their interpersonal boundaries. Being aware of and working with these interpersonal boundaries are features of family work (Lam 1991), although as we explained in Chapter 1 (Introduction), we are not aiming to deliver systemic family therapy.

Boundaries provide a limit: they are the lines around the system to which individuals belong. These lines are not physically drawn (in the way that lines appear on a tennis court to inform the progress of the game), but are communicated through overt and/or covert means by the individuals involved; they may or may not be obvious to an outside observer. Indeed, it is more often than not the case that the rules are unwritten, yet they exert a strong influence on the roles that individual family members take on and they develop as the family moves on both physically and emotionally. It is also important to note that boundaries are never constant, but change continually according to the demands on the system that they surround.

We know that any mental illness can put tremendous strain on a family system (Leff 1998). Moreover, it is possible that psychosis exerts a particular pressure because of its impact on the service user's sense of reality, including his or her ability to interact with others as previously expected. Interestingly, it has been shown that if a strain is put on any system for a period of time, then that system will begin to change in order to maintain the status quo, through a process known as **homeostasis** (Guttman 1981). Unfortunately this phenomenon (which is well recognised by engineers and biologists) is not usually acknowledged by mental health workers, although it can usefully illuminate some of the ways in which we see families under pressure behaving.

The stresses and strains on a family system caused by mental illness often lead family members to feel that everything is out of control. Then gradually, as it adapts to the traumatic situation, a family may begin to tighten its boundaries and become more rigid (which is another phenomenon well known in the engineering world, such as when a bridge becomes brittle as it tightens up under the influence of ongoing stress). Similarly, a family system that finds itself under constant pressure is likely to respond with rules and roles becoming more fixed and communication that is increasingly 'brittle' or stilted.

As a means of trying to cope, it is possible that what can be described as a 'no talk' rule comes into operation within a family which fears that talking about problems will further disturb the system. Indeed, you may be familiar with the figure of speech 'least said, soonest mended', which is another way of expressing the same rule. However, these rules are not generally conscious, but develop intuitively through the individual's efforts to cope with their difficult situation. As family workers you may hear a family member saying, 'We don't like to talk about it' when considering the service user's mental illness or resulting problems; or they may demonstrate this rule in action by refusing to discuss their situation. This rule and the rigid boundaries that may accompany it therefore require family workers to be extremely sensitive when they attempt to offer help, as there is a strong likelihood that family members at this point are not ready (or cannot imagine that it is possible) to change their patterns of coping. For this reason, they can appear hostile as they try to defend themselves (individually or collectively) and are quite likely to refuse any intervention if it is perceived as a threat or a waste of time. There is also a risk that mental health workers fail to properly acknowledge the family's trauma and somehow think that this current pattern is the way the family has always been, even making judgements about impact on the service user of growing up in this system – a judgement that is probably far from the truth. An understanding of how rigid boundaries can develop and the purpose they serve will offer family workers another way to view this kind of situation.

Alternatively, roles and rules may become haphazard and communication diffuse in the confusion of trying to cope with the traumatic events associated with mental illness. A family may not be able to contain its distress; in such instances family workers will observe a 'spilling out' of problems, beyond a family's usual boundaries. It can be that no one really knows who is doing what within this type of family situation, with family members often taking on each other's roles, such as when a service user's sibling takes on a parental role with the service user and/or their parents, when the parents are failing to enact their rightful responsibilities. A good demonstration of these diffuse boundaries is shown in the television sitcom *Absolutely Fabulous*, in which the daughter of one of the main characters has adopted a parental stance with her mother, while the mother and her friend behave in a quite childlike manner. Neither mother nor daughter appears very satisfied in her role, as they are very critical of each other, showing that it is not usually comfortable to live within a diffuse boundary.

The types of boundary described above are those that family workers are most likely to come across when they meet families in distress. However, there are families that generally manage to maintain clear boundaries despite the problems associated with coping with psychosis, so family workers should never presume they will need to work with service users and carers on boundary issues. Nonetheless, it is useful to remember the possibilities, as listed in Box 9.2 and be aware of their possible impact.

Box 9.2 Types of boundary that can exist within family systems

Boundaries that occur within a family system can include:

- rigid
- diffuse
- clear
- a combination of all three.

When their boundaries are clear the service user and carers can most effectively explore the usefulness of the information offered to them and employ it flexibly. This clarity allows each member of the system to recognise what is expected of him or her in their particular role and communicate it to others.

It is unlikely that any family will have constantly clear boundaries as the stresses within a system are forever changing, so in reality there will probably be a mix of the various types of boundary, with one showing more predominantly at any one time. It is often the case that when a family's boundaries become more rigid it is in response to their attempts to attain more clarity and control; diffuse boundaries tend to be an attempt by family members to dissipate the tensions in order to survive their struggles on a day-to-day basis.

To family workers, both rigid and diffuse boundaries may feel quite frustrating, as they can feel somewhat like barriers. However, by understanding the resistance that we experience from time to time in the context of a family's boundaries, and appreciating that what we are meeting are natural coping mechanisms within that family system, we can begin to work with them. This frame of reference allows us to explore the boundaries and examine their usefulness, through finding out what the illness has meant to the different members of the family, what they understand and how they have managed to date. We can then go on (without criticism) to explore where these boundaries may have indeed become a barrier to developing further coping strategies. So rather than push against the barrier and risk alienating ourselves from the service user and/or carers, we can accept what we are experiencing and use it to find out more about the family system.

In practice it may be useful for family workers who find themselves meeting a barrier or resistance to review what they know from the initial family work assessments in response to the following questions.

- What are the carers' and service user's beliefs about the illness?
- What has been successful for them in trying to cope?
- What strategies appear unhelpful or damaging?
- What support (if any) do they appear to think or feel they need?

Assessments such as the Relative Assessment Interview (RAI – Barrowclough and Tarrier 1997) and the Knowledge About Schizophrenia Interview (KASI – Barrowclough *et al.* 1987) as described in Chapter 8 (How to Conduct Family Work Assessments) are well suited to gathering the answers we seek.

Miller and Rollnick (1991) have coined the phrase 'roll with resistance' (p.59), which we feel perfectly captures the essence of acknowledging and working with resistance. We find it particularly valuable, because it recognises that, within this resistance, there is energy and motivation that can be used beneficially, if this energy is not wasted by the individual concerned feeling that they have to defend their position. By rolling with the resistance, you avoid provoking a defensive response, thus making it possible to explore the intent behind the resistance (which is likely to be something to do with maintaining a feeling of safety within some kind of status quo or familiar situation). Indeed, the resistance may fulfil an important function in the communication patterns of a family system. Helping service users and carers to make sense of their behaviour patterns and boundaries, by encouraging them to tell their story, then sharing knowledge and going on to solve problems together brings the possibility of a choice in the type of boundary adopted. This can then alter all family members' experiences, with the likelihood that they feel safer within their communication with each other.

Drawing a genogram

You will see that the first page of our FWA form is designed to contain a brief family history and for this we suggest using a genogram (McGoldrich, Gerson and Shellenberger 1999) to succinctly capture the relevant details in a very accessible format. Some family workers (especially, we find, those coming from a social services rather than a health service background) will be familiar with the use of this tool, but for those to whom it is new we have included an explanation of its purpose and details of how to draw one.

A genogram is really just a family tree that includes social data to make it useful as a brief pictorial representation of the family's history. It can provide a map of the family across many generations that records any major events experienced by the family, including the losses of various family members and at what age. Where various family members live (or lived), their occupations and how much time they spend in each other's company can be recorded, as well as the known patterns of communication, including whether relationships are considered **enmeshed** or **estranged**.

All that is needed to draw a genogram is a large piece of paper, something to write clearly with and an individual's willingness to contribute what they know or believe to be true. Indeed it is often the discussion among family members about their differing perspectives of the family's history that makes this such a rich process and a good place to encourage the service user and carers to develop the habit of coming to a shared understanding of an event. For genograms to be most useful it is important to avoid overcrowding them by having too much information crammed into too small a space, which is why we suggest starting with a large piece of paper. The large scale also promotes the intention that this is a shared exercise, as it is possible for a number of people to work on it together when they can all see what they are doing. The finished diagram may then be reduced in size for ease of storage as long as its clarity is not lost.

The symbols used within a genogram follow the conventions for drawing a family tree:

- a male is represented by a square
- a female is represented by a circle
- if the sex of a person is unknown he or she is represented by a triangle (this is mostly used when there is a lack of clarity about the sex of a stillborn baby or in circumstances when there is a lack of exact knowledge about a large number of a grandparent's or great grandparent's siblings)
- a marital pair is indicated by a line drawn from the square to the circle, with the date of the marriage written along the line

- offspring are entered according to age, starting with the oldest on the left
- individuals' ages are written within the symbol that represents them.

A married couple with three children is illustrated by the genogram in Figure 9.1, showing an older son followed by a set of twins.

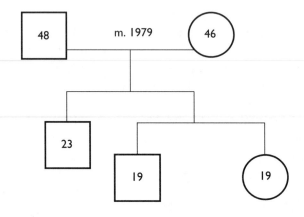

Figure 9.1 Example of a genogram of a typical family

Further details can be recorded as follows:

- a double line through the line of the previous marriage (including the date if possible) portrays a divorce
- drawing a cross through their symbol indicates a family member no longer living; including the year of death is useful if it is known.

Thus, a more complex, but not untypical, family may be represented in a genogram as shown in Figure 9.2.

It is useful to draw a dotted line around, or colour in, the symbols of the family members who compose the household with whom you are working, as shown in Figure 9.2.

A genogram may also contain facts (or supposed facts) about the health and causes of death of various family members. This can sometimes elicit detail of a family member who was diagnosed with schizophrenia or who was perhaps known within the family as being 'rather odd', thereby providing an opening for family workers to discuss the possible genetic predisposition to developing psychosis and explore the family's views on this. This may lead to some family members discovering details of relatives they never knew existed, so you should be prepared to cope with surprises when facilitating this exercise.

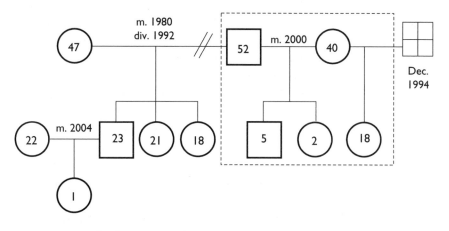

Figure 9.2 Example of a genogram of a more complex, but not untypical, family

Keeping notes of family meetings

When doing family work as a mental health worker employed by statutory services you will need to consider how you will keep records of all your interactions with each family member. From the assessments that you and your co-worker have already completed you will probably have amassed a large amount of paperwork and this may already have necessitated some discussion with the service user's care coordinator and possibly his or her mental health team manager regarding where this information should be kept. You may also have to consider the fact that the service user's carers are not technically mental health service users themselves: different services have differing protocols relating to how the information about carers is held. This matter is somewhat complicated in Britain by the National Service Framework (NSF) for Mental Health (DH 1999) requirement for carers to have an assessment of their own needs and a care plan devised to meet these identified needs. Further to this, in some places the standard of mental health services is judged by whether or not this (among a range of other criteria) is being achieved. Against their success in meeting these criteria service providers receive a rating of the quality of their services, so accurate records that can be audited are obviously required. There is no simple answer to this, but it is an issue that you need to resolve within your own service structure, to ensure that you are keeping the information you gather from all family members in a legally acceptable as well as practically useful way.

The requirement for all carers 'who provide regular and substantial care for a person on CPA' (DH 1999, p.69) to have their needs assessed as advocated by Standard 6 of the NSF has not generally been well received by mental health workers in statutory services in Britain. Nevertheless, we are aware of one statutory service in the Brighton and Hove area that has had 100 per cent success in meeting this standard, demonstrating that it can be done with minimal dedicated resources. Various assessment tools, such as the Carers' and Users' Expectations of Services (Lelliot *et al.* 2001) and the Experience of Caregiving Inventory (Szmukler *et al.* 1996), have been suggested as means to conduct these carers' assessments. Indeed the mental health trusts in which we work in the counties of Avon, Gloucestershire and Wiltshire have created their own carers' assessment tools based on these tools, as has **Rethink**. However, despite the care that went into creating these assessments, they are very long and have not been found easy to use. So even with strong encouragement (such as in the Avon and Wiltshire Mental Health Partnership NHS Trust (AWP) where Gina is employed to champion the recognition of carers' needs, while appreciating the important roles they fulfil), there has been a low uptake of carers' assessments in practice. In response to these difficulties, carers working on behalf of AWP devised a shorter assessment tool (shown here in Appendix 6) that, like the RAI (Barrowclough and Tarrier 1997), is intended to be conducted in a conversational style, to try to promote and normalise the practice of talking to carers and routinely assessing their needs within statutory mental health services. Its use is proving more popular than that of its predecessor (which has been retained as a follow-up assessment where greater detail is required), so we feel able to commend its use to others even though it has not been formally **validated**.

Having established a protocol for keeping family work notes within their own practice area, it is useful to think about what family workers actually need to record. In practice we have found it useful to have a standardised recognisable form containing the date when the meeting took place, the names of everyone present and what was planned. It is then useful to record both the content of the discussions and how the process took place, including the interactions and alliances between various individuals. Any outcomes, plans and/or homework tasks, as well as goals for future meetings, should also be carefully noted, along with the date of the next meeting when progress will be reviewed. The form used in AWP is shown in Appendix 10 to illustrate how such a document may be structured.

Some family workers prefer to have the notes completed during the actual family meeting, possibly drawing on a Quaker model of collaborative practice (Attwood *et al.* 2003) that allows all those present to agree the content at the time. Others prefer to take brief notes during the meeting and complete a fuller record within the next 24 hours, which can then be shared with all concerned and amended as required. Either way, the tasks of writing and distributing the notes may be allocated to one of the family workers or any family member; it is useful to switch this responsibility from meeting to meeting to foster a shared ownership of its value.

An additional document that may be useful in practice, depending on the willingness of family members to complete it, is known as the 'Helpful Aspects of Therapy' form (Kuipers *et al.* 2002 p.133). There are two versions of this: one for family members and one for workers; as the name suggests it provides an opportunity for individuals to record what they have found helpful within the family meeting. Comments captured on these forms can often be built upon in future meetings.

It is worth encouraging the family to retain their own copy of all the shared family work documentation in a place that is accessible to them all (or if communication is poor and/or trust lacking, for individuals to maintain their own separate copies). Our aim here is to promote the idea that they are likely to benefit from keeping a record of what has been helpful and/or unhelpful to refer back to as they develop their coping strategies. It can also be useful to store educational materials in the same place so that they may be consulted as necessary, alongside a copy of the service user's latest care plan and relapse prevention plan (Smith 2000).

Length and frequency of family meetings

The length of family meetings and how often they take place is likely to vary considerably between one family and another, with an initial agreement about it being made when formulating the ground rules. The family should already understand from your introductory conversations that family work does not go on indefinitely, so if you feel that this is unclear it may help to reiterate the point. This should ensure that discussing the length and frequency of meetings takes place within a context which recognises that the time spent together is a valuable resource to be used wisely.

Service users and carers may ask your advice on how often to meet. We find there is no single answer to this question as it needs to be a response to the business to be addressed during the meetings. For example, if you are helping the family cope with a crisis or carers are close to collapse you may visit once a week to set short-term goals to try to rectify the situation. However, if the pace of change is likely to be slow it is more appropriate to meet every two to four weeks, as meeting too often can add pressure by looking for progress before new strategies have had time to have an impact.

The length of a family meeting will depend largely on the service user's ability to engage in the process. We find if he or she is having difficulty concentrating it is better to keep the meeting short, which may mean as little as 10 to 15 minutes and gradually build it up towards an hour. In such cases it may also be useful to schedule a break in the middle of the meeting to extend the overall time spent together in a manageable way.

We do not usually find it productive to meet for longer than an hour as most individuals (including the family workers) begin to lose focus beyond this length of time. An exception to this may be necessary if one or more carers are travelling a long distance to attend the meeting, in which case it will probably be appropriate to have longer less frequent meetings. If working in this situation you will need to take particular care to ensure that the service user is not overwhelmed, and you should probably still try to avoid going on beyond two hours. If meetings are scheduled to be longer than one hour we definitely recommend taking a break at some point within them.

Family work skills and competences

There are a number of skills and competences identified within the Family Work Skills Checklist (FWSC) devised by Devane and colleagues (1998), which particularly relate to ensuring that family meetings are well structured and thereby increase the likelihood that they will be effective. Others relate to the specific skills that form the basis of the collaborative process that underpins the whole philosophy of family work. In the following section we will discuss some of these skills and competences in detail and explain their relevance fully. For further reference, a complete version of the FWSC is included here as Appendix 8.

Agenda setting and controlling a family meeting

It may help you to think of a family meeting as being very similar to any business meeting such as your employer's board meetings. However, there is a crucial difference in that the emotional content of a family meeting is likely to be painful at times to the family members present, so the person chairing the meeting as well as other participants will need to take account of the impact this will have; business meetings are rather less likely to evoke such a personal response. There is a further difference, which relates to the handling of emotions: in business meetings the emotional content of an agenda item is often not addressed overtly, although its influence may still be felt; in a family meeting the emotional issues are fully recognised as being central to the process. For this reason several items within the FWSC relate directly to the worker's ability to elicit and manage emotions.

The way in which family meetings most resemble other business meetings is through the use of an agenda to structure the way in which participants spend their time together. To be most useful in a family meeting this agenda is drawn up by one of the workers (or possibly a family member once the process has become familiar) inviting everyone to suggest items he or she wishes to cover during the meeting. These items are then discussed briefly to allow a shared decision to be made about which should take priority and how much time should be allocated to each one. The task of keeping to the agenda is then allocated either to a chairperson alone or divided between this individual, who will concentrate on the content of the discussion (by inviting everyone to contribute and checking that their points are understood) and another, who will take charge of time keeping.

Nevertheless, at times (despite good planning) it may be impossible to completely discuss all the items included on a family meeting's agenda. In such cases any unfinished business should be clearly acknowledged and rescheduled for attention at a future meeting.

A further skill that family workers need to develop is that of limiting the discussion of irrelevant issues without causing offence, to maintain the focus on the agenda items. It is then important to encourage individuals to look at each item in sufficient depth to reach some satisfactory resolution within the resources available.

Interpersonal skills

When concentrating on learning a new skill it is not uncommon for mental health workers to forget to maintain their usual interpersonal skills. To ensure that family workers do not ignore the importance of offering family intervention within the context of a sound therapeutic relationship a number of these interpersonal skills are specifically noted on the FWSC. These include demonstrating a relaxed confidence, and showing warmth and concern, while avoiding any interaction that could convey hostility, ridicule or condescension. It is for this reason that we encourage you to practise any new family work skills in the classroom or supervision before attempting to use them with a family in need.

Checking and negotiating

In Chapter 7 (How to Prepare for Family Work Meetings) we explained the term modelling and its use within family interventions. By using this technique workers may demonstrate the skills necessary to explore alternative points of view and reach agreement, maintaining a flexible and open stance that respects everyone's position. Over time, it is hoped that this way of communicating will be adopted by all family members whenever they discuss potentially contentious or emotionally arousing issues.

Through the family work assessment process we hope to have gained a fairly wide perspective of what the service user and carers are coping with and how they have managed to overcome difficulties in the past, which may help us to feel able to make many suggestions that could lead to improvements in the quality of individual's lives. However, it is vital we remember that the responsibility for making changes lies with the family members and we must never presume that we know best. Instead we should always check that we have understood an individual's meaning correctly and, when changes appear necessary, negotiate with all concerned how the hoped-for outcome may be achieved.

Giving and receiving feedback

A particularly important family work skill involves grasping the main points of what the service user and/or carers are saying as well as picking up the subtle connotations of anything else that may be being expressed less directly. This requires you to check that you have properly understood an individual's meaning by offering a summary of what you have heard (that is neither too literal nor tangential) and asking others to correct you if necessary. You also need to be able to ask whether an intervention by yourself or others has been helpful or not in order to plan the best way to proceed and capitalise on the lessons learned. It is therefore crucial that you become comfortable with giving and receiving both positive and negative feedback explicitly; some principles that will help you to achieve this are covered in detail in Chapter 7 (How to Prepare for Family Work Meetings).

Setting and reviewing homework

Much of the benefit that service users and carers derive from family work comes from practising the skills they have learned during family meetings with each other outside of these meetings (Falloon *et al.* 1993). Despite this knowledge, many new family workers have difficulty with the concept of homework and therefore fail to embrace it as part of the family work process. Indeed, from our experience as trainers and supervisors we feel that workers sometimes communicate their disquiet to family members and consequently meet resistance from a family when trying to introduce it. We therefore urge you to work through any prejudices you may have relating to the issue of homework with your co-worker and/or supervisor to ensure that your own feelings do not block its use.

Interestingly we find that some family members have the same negative initial response to the notion of homework as some new family workers. Therefore having worked through his or her own barriers a worker will be well placed to help a service user or carer do the same. It is important not to underestimate the value of this type of interaction because although it may not relate directly to the immediate concerns of coping with psychosis, it clearly demonstrates the worker's wish to establish a truly collaborative working relationship. Some (safe) personal disclosure from a worker to one or more family members simply enhances the process (Drage *et al.* 2004).

Having gained an agreement with family members that homework (or what-ever you choose to call it) is a vital component of family work you need to use it wisely. This means never setting a homework task without a purpose; and having agreed a purpose, it will usually be shared with all concerned. However, this is not the same as having a predetermined outcome; homework tasks are often expressed as an experiment that may inform future interventions.

Whatever the set homework task, it is essential that everybody involved in it understands what is expected of him or her and everyone else. To avoid any risk of confusion we generally recommend making a written note of the homework during the family meeting where it is agreed, including its purpose, the exact details of the task and when it will be reviewed. The number of items relating to it in the FWSC underscores the importance of this detail.

Education within family intervention

The blaming culture that exists within many societies worldwide has led some families to believe that they are the cause of the service user's psychosis, or at least partly to blame. In some other cases (although the accusations seem unfair) carers have felt blamed by others for their relative's mental illness. For this reason, much of our work with families involves an educative process to try to correct these misconceptions, right from our very first meeting with any member of the service user's family, whenever this takes place.

As we have said before, the overall aim of family work is to create a partner-ship in which alliances can be formed between all parties, recognising their individual experiences and contributions that promote recovering from psycho-sis. This involves valuing all contributions to the education process, however different they may be from our own views as family workers. It is important for us to try to integrate the varying perspectives to come to a shared understanding that provides a platform for further shared learning. This should foster the collabora-tion through which resources may be pooled to try to overcome any difficulties that have arisen through the experience of psychosis, using the normalising ratio-nale of a stress vulnerability model as far as possible, to help individuals make sense of their position.

It is usual for the initial educationally focused family meetings to help pro-vide a rationale and framework for the other components of family intervention. For this reason, it is important that any information about psychosis is not given to carers in isolation. As we discussed in Chapter 5 (When to Offer Family Work for Psychosis), although families may well be requesting information about psy-chosis from any mental health workers they meet, in our experience giving it out of context can actually block future engagement in family interventions. There-fore a request by carers for information should prompt a referral for family work so that they get what they want as soon as possible, as well as an opportunity to meet needs they have not yet acknowledged.

The family work education process traditionally focuses on helping carers to understand more about schizophrenia (Kuipers *et al.* 2002), to enhance their skills, and/or developing the service user's understanding of his or her own experience of psychosis, facilitating opportunities to foster a working understanding of the illness within the family (Falloon *et al.* 1984). However, before we go on to expand this aspect of education within family interventions, we would like to remind you of another facet, which is quite likely to precede that, which involves encouraging the service user to tell their story.

Bearing in mind that the need for family work is often provoked by a psychotic relapse or other crisis, the service user is unlikely to be able to fully share information at first (often due to a distorted sense of reality). At this point it is far more likely that carers will be a source of information for the mental health workers providing the service user's care. Unfortunately some service providers get themselves caught in a misunderstanding of the issue of confidentiality at this stage, feeling that they are unable to talk to carers without the service user's permission, and because of his or her psychosis this permission is often not forthcoming. However, in our experience it is much more usual in the early stages of a first episode or relapse of psychosis that carers will want to report what they know in order to contribute to the care plan, rather than receive information. Therefore there is no problem, as workers are not disclosing any confidential information. Indeed, carers are generally keen to share constructive aspects of their caring roles and responsibilities (Schene, Tessler and Gamache 1996), as well as provide details of the difficulties they and the service user have been facing. This we suggest is in most cases the beginning of the education process.

When immersed in the education process it is easy for family workers and carers to presume that the more the service user discusses his or her experience of psychosis, the more insight will be gained and the sooner recovery will be achieved. However, this is not always the case: it may actually be that increased insight is linked to an increased risk of depression and therefore a greater risk of suicide (Birchwood *et al.* 1993). Family workers must therefore remain mindful that a service user's unwillingness to acknowledge their diagnosis may have a protective function that should not be brutally removed. Nonetheless, **integrating** the psychotic experience can be associated with better outcomes (Spencer, Murray and Plaistow 2000), so gentle exploration of the service user's understanding of his or her symptoms should (in most cases) be encouraged.

It has been shown that a full psycho-education package (as advocated by Falloon *et al.* 1984) appears to increase psychotic relapse rates for service users living in families where carers are already exhibiting low-EE behaviours (Linszen *et al.* 1996), although there seems to be a tendency for families to drop out of interventions that they feel go on too long (Leff *et al.* 1982), which may in itself have a self-protective function. In any case, these findings emphasise the importance of ensuring that interventions are tailored to meet the needs of each family. Sharing information should never be formulaic and, as family workers, you will need to consider what education is necessary and likely to be useful for the particular family with whom you are working before providing any new material.

The education process in family work is not an academic exercise. It is really an opportunity for the service user and carers to gain a deeper understanding of the service user's personal experience of psychosis and for them to have an opportunity to learn to interpret behaviours they associate with the illness, which previously they have had no means to construe. Encouraging the service user to discuss his or her experiences of psychosis is best achieved by promoting their acceptance of their position as the person who knows most about those experiences. If this is accepted it is then possible for carers to ask their questions, and for the service user to explain the thoughts behind their disturbed or apparently odd behaviour, from a position of authority that may boost his or her self-esteem, which can then engender recovery.

The increased level of understanding by all concerned gained through the family work education process can then become the basis for further family and/or individual interventions. We recognise that some families may not require anything more than this education component of family work. However, this is not the same as offering only education, which was found to be ineffective (Tarrier *et al.* 1988), as the family work assessments will still have been completed and the need for other elements will have been considered. The service user and carers will also know what else is available so can re-refer themselves for further family intervention should the need arise.

Working with emotions

Gaining an understanding of the service user's psychosis, and in particular the recognition that previously unintelligible behaviours are actually signs of a diagnosable mental illness, can be extremely upsetting for carers; this is often most apparent immediately following the formal application of a diagnostic term. For example, a parent may have used criticism to try to motivate his daughter before her lack of drive was acknowledged to be part of a first episode of psychosis (EPPIC, 1997), so feels guilty for this unjust behaviour when the diagnosis is made. We therefore feel it is vital within our work with families not only to acknowledge the feelings of each family member, but also to encourage their expression so that we can work with these emotions overtly rather than deal with their covert impact.

From our experience as family work trainers and supervisors we have created a list (shown in Box 9.3) of the emotions that family workers have seen many carers express in response to their relative's psychosis, to help us notice common themes and consider appropriate family interventions. What this list demonstrates is that most of these emotions are also expressed and/or felt by people who have experienced bereavement caused by a death.

Box 9.3 Emotions expressed by carers during family interventions

Shock	Feeling trapped
Loss	Uselessness
Grief	Jealousy
Fear	Relief
Worry	Resentment
Denial	Stigmatisation
Apprehension	Depression
Sadness	Loneliness
Guilt	Powerlessness
Feeling of isolation	Blame of others and/or oneself
Anger	Hurt
Anxiety	

To date there is little research in this area, but there are emerging findings to suggest that coming to terms with the death of a family member and coping with a relative's psychotic illness are in some ways similar. To explore this in great depth is beyond the scope of this manual, but we will briefly describe a few studies to demonstrate our point.

- Karp and Tanarugsachock (2000) conducted a qualitative study to explore the ways the emotional responses of carers of people suffering from a severe mental illness changed as the service user's illness evolved by doing a **thematic analysis** of the content of a number of **semi-structured interviews** undertaken with these carers. They found that carers tended to experience fear, anxiety and confusion prior to the service user receiving a diagnosis, apparently compounded by 'their impulse to deny that the problem was mental illness' (p.12). Guilt was then common immediately after the diagnosis was confirmed, particularly in children of the person with schizophrenia, and seemed to be associated with having doubted that their parent was ill. This shows that a carer's feelings are likely to be different at various stages of the service user's psychosis, from first signs through to recovery, so any education offered to families must take this into account. A further point of interest from this study was that a lack of clarity from professionals with regard to diagnosis and prognosis compounded carers' difficulties. This lack of clarity can be seen as adding to the factors that block family members from moving on to accommodate the feelings of loss within their **psychological transition**.

- A study conducted by Miller *et al.* (1990) focused on families of chronically mentally ill service users whose diagnoses included bipolar disorder, depression, personality disorders and schizophrenia. Family members in this study displayed higher levels of continued grieving than those who had suffered a death in the family.

- A study by Atkinson (1994) compared the grief reactions of three carer groups: parents who had lost their child through death; those with a child suffering from chronic schizophrenia; and parents whose child was left with an organic personality disorder following a head injury. It was a well-conducted study that included 25 families in each group. The results showed that the pattern of grief for parents of a son or daughter with schizophrenia is quite different from the pattern in other groups. It appeared that coping with a child's death or personality disorder led to high levels of grief initially and these tended to subside over time. Conversely, the initial response to schizophrenia showed a comparatively low level of grieving, but this increased and became chronic as the condition persisted. These results were thought to be due to the ongoing, fluctuating course of schizophrenia, which makes it harder to accommodate than death or a personality disorder, as these are both final outcomes.

- A study at Ashworth Hospital (McCann, McKeown and Porter 1996) reported a finding that guilt and depression in the relatives of those experiencing schizophrenia correlated with a lack of knowledge about the cause of the illness, which led to them blaming themselves.

These studies suggest that grief is very prevalent among individuals living with psychosis, so needs to be addressed within our family interventions.

If we look at this in terms of psychological transitions (Parkes 1998), the parent of a child who has died has a clearer transition to make over time. This clear transition does not occur when living with someone who has a chronic illness, so uncertainty is experienced that leaves the carer in a constant state of transition. William Bridges (2003) found this phenomenon while working with organisations; his findings suggest that, within the transition from the old position to the new one, there is a period when everything is in a state of flux. Feelings are intensified during this period, which has the effect for those within the experience of feeling as if they are in a war zone. When the experience is finally reconciled, a move towards new tasks that accommodate the losses is made and consequently the intensity of feelings subsides. From this we can begin to appreciate why the carer of a person with psychosis who remains in a state of uncertainty will experience an intensification of feelings over time.

Psychosis, with its characteristic pattern of acute episodes and periods of remission, means the family is faced with an ongoing threat of change. So within our family interventions it is important that we remember the impact of this uncertainty as we try to promote the development of new coping strategies. Finkelman (2000) describes this lack of control over their own future plans following the service user's diagnosis of psychosis, suffered by all family members, as a further loss in itself; this additional source of grief should be acknowledged and worked with. This may take place within family meetings although in our experience while this is usually appropriate for the service user, carers are more likely to express their grief in another forum, away from the service user.

Working with loss and grief

Lafond (2002) suggests that 'the primary focus of mental health professionals is *treating the illness in individuals,* but they do not usually recognize or treat the illness *as loss*' (p.8 – italics in original). We do not feel that this applies to us as family workers, but serves to remind us that recognising the impact of loss and subsequent grieving should be central to our interventions. Having already provided some descriptions of grief in Chapter 3 (Why Offer Family Work for Psychosis?) we will not repeat these definitions here, but instead concentrate on how to work with loss and grief appropriately within family work.

Despite the common occurrence of the feelings associated with grief exhibited by carers and service users coping with psychosis, in our experience it is not routinely explored explicitly by most mental health workers. This view is echoed by Lafond (2002), who found that 'rarely will psychiatrists or mental health practitioners talk to…family members about the experience of loss related to mental illness' (p.7). From our search of the relevant literature it does not appear that carers are unwilling to discuss their feelings: many depict their position with heart-wrenching clarity. For example, a young woman describing her feelings towards her brother, ten years after he was first diagnosed with schizophrenia, vividly illustrates the strong connection between burden and grief:

> I can now see him without fear, but not without sorrow. The chronic nature of the illness makes it a problem that is never truly resolved, and the sadness I feel about the bleakness of his life is a burden I still carry around like invisible baggage. (Brodoff 1988, p.116)

This suggests family workers should be prepared to open up this topic for discussion within the RAI (Barrowclough and Tarrier 1997) and take it forward with gentle prompting as appropriate.

Finkelman (2000) describes 'an experience of dual loss of the person who was and the person who might have been' (p.144), and usefully clarifies that this 'is not an issue of the dashing of parental expectations'. Instead it is an empathic grief for the service user who is also grieving. Karp and Tanarugsachock (2000) also found that relatives suffered from a chronic sorrow in response to loss of the person they knew pre-illness, but 'once beyond their profound loss [came] to a deep admiration and respect for their family members who bravely struggle with the unimaginable pain of mental illness' (p.22).

Angermeyer and Matschinger (1996) found that families tended to experience less guilt in relation to the service user if they held a biological rather than a psychosocial view of the illness. This is important to remember when proffering educative material in family meetings, and may explain why some carers are so strongly wedded to a medicalised view of psychosis and its treatment options.

In her book *Grieving Mental Illnesses*, Virginia Lafond (2002) notes that carers often feel at a loss to know what to do 'which can lead to hopelessness and helplessness' (p.20) and, as discussed earlier, this could be because they are constantly at the point of loss (which includes a loss of certainty) due to the unpredictable nature of psychosis. Unlike the case of death, with its finality, the ongoing potential episodes of psychosis cause the carer to continually feel the loss experience and/or continually feel at a loss. Lafond also observes that a carer often has many losses to cope with, such as their career, their marriage, family life as they knew it, their social life, the relationship they previously experienced with the service user, and so on. That the impact is so wide ranging may help us as family workers to comprehend what is preventing a carer and service user from their expressing grief. This difficulty in expressing the grief is especially common when the loss is not generally recognised (such as it would be following the death of a child) or is compounded by stigma. The expression of grief may also be suppressed by the carer's fear of upsetting the service user and thereby adding to the severity of their illness. This difficult situation is well summarised by Lafond (1998), who notes that 'mental illness and its attendant losses meet the criteria for disenfranchized loss, in that this loss remains unrecognized by society, with neither the rituals nor language of mourning, grieved in isolation, often in shame and stigma' (p.237–238).

However, once the loss is acknowledged it becomes possible for the healthy process of grieving to begin. Indeed, through this process, an individual may rekindle a feeling of hopefulness and begin to make positive choices for the future (Lafond, 2002). We may or may not choose to share these insights with service users and carers within our family interventions, but we hope they will help you maintain your therapeutic optimism as you pool your resources with those of families coping with psychosis.

Normalising emotional responses

An important function of family workers is to try to help both the service user and carers normalise their emotional reactions. A lack of acknowledgement of their emotions can lead to a feeling of frustration and tension or the possibility that family members disconnect from the family work process. If emotions are explored without normalising them this can lead to individuals feeling guilty, as carers and the service user struggle to express negative feelings. In order to begin this process of normalisation in family work we have found that it is extremely useful to use the phrase: 'It is understandable that...' when we encourage family members to express their feelings. This enables the emotion to be understood within the context that it is being expressed and should help to reduce a service user's or carer's unjustified sense of guilt.

There are some **schemas** (listed in Box 9.4) that may help you to recognise what underlies the emotional responses you are most likely to see in family meetings. It is always important for family workers to acknowledge these emotions as they arise and to be prepared to reschedule some agenda items if necessary in order to do so.

When a parent or spouse has to alter their usual perception of their loved one and/or cannot express their love in the usual way and have it received as such, then understandably they may grieve. If a sister feels that she can no longer relate to her sibling in the same way as before, acknowledging what they had and what they could have had can feel like a tremendous loss and, understandably, she may grieve.

Many carers and families do not understand what psychosis is and therefore feel confused. Understandably this sort of confusion can be frightening. Families develop their own individual systems as they progress, which have all sorts of overt and covert ways of being with each other that include their values, rules,

---

Box 9.4 Schema that may help to normalise emotional responses

It is normal that when:

- the expression of love has been blocked, one grieves
- a family does not understand the illness, members often experience fear
- a family's normal way of being together is blocked, they may feel angry.

---

accepted mannerisms and expectations. If these are suddenly blocked or changed radically without negotiation then, understandably, some family members may become angry.

These are all normal reactions to an abnormal situation. The conditions created by the illness are not usually within the normal experiences of family life so individuals are bound to deal with their new situation in the best way they can with the resources they have available. Family workers can bring additional resources (without criticism) that may promote new ways of coping.

To work with emotions, you and your co-worker first need to be willing and able to acknowledge your own emotions, as being emotionally unaware can limit your responses towards emotions that are being expressed by others in family meetings. You need to be able to show some confidence in handling others' emotions without becoming overwhelmed; being able to manage your own is an important aspect of this. However, managing your own emotions is not synonymous with not showing any emotional response when in the company of a service user and/or carer. You will undoubtedly hear some sad things as a family worker and family members appreciate that you are able to show a human response to these (Drage *et al.* 2004). Nonetheless, it is important that you are not overcome by emotion to such an extent that you are unable to meet a family member's needs.

As family workers we have found that debriefing immediately after a family work meeting with our co-worker is invaluable when working with the strong emotions expressed openly or non-verbally by family members. Moreover, if you find that your emotional response is obstructing your interventions with a particular family then it is vital to access family work supervision as soon as possible.

We recognise that working with families in distress can be emotionally draining (as well as extremely rewarding) so normalising our own emotions is important too!

Summary

The business of family meetings should always relate to the reasons why a family was initially referred for intervention, and build on the material gathered through the family work assessments. This will include pooling the resources of all concerned and maximising the service user's and carers' strengths to meet the family members' needs and work towards their goals.

To be most effective family meetings need to be well organised through a shared agenda and to take place within an agreed time frame. Although the length and frequency of meetings may vary between one family and another, these parameters will relate to the family's needs in all cases. It is useful to keep a written record of the discussions that have taken place during every family meeting, including details of any plans and/or decisions made. The family work process is enhanced further if all those involved complete tasks and practise their skills outside of the meeting; the lessons learned from this homework can then be used to inform future interventions. A list of negotiated ground rules is also likely to facilitate the smooth running of family meetings, thereby increasing their effectiveness.

Workers need to balance their ability to provide a safe structure within family meetings with a relaxed confidence, which guards them against becoming too directive. Negotiation skills are therefore crucial to developing the collaborative relationships needed to deliver family interventions effectively.

The ways that family workers talk with service users and carers should always convey a genuine interest in them and their situation. By practising new skills in the classroom or within supervision sessions workers are most likely to maintain their interpersonal skills when delivering unfamiliar family interventions in practice.

Acknowledging and working with emotions is a vital component of our integrated family work model. Recognising the schema underlying carers' and service users' emotional responses to psychosis will help family workers to be most effective. Grief is a particularly common response to the experience of psychosis, although mental health workers often ignore it. Family workers need to buck this trend and encourage both their colleagues and family members to accept and work with the losses associated with psychosis in order to achieve an optimistic view of a future that embraces recovery.

Key points

- It is as important to work to promote service users' and carers' strengths, as well as helping them to overcome their problems and meet their needs.

- Family workers should have a good grasp of individuals' assets following the assessment process to enable them to encourage all resources to be shared.

- Collaboratively agreed ground rules support the smooth running of family work meetings and supervision sessions, which have much in common.

- Agreeing and working to a set agenda helps to make the best use of time spent in family meetings.

- Helping family members to recognise the roles and responsibilities they adopt enables them to choose whether or not it is useful to maintain these positions.

- It can be useful to help family members recognise the boundaries that exist between themselves, as well as the boundary between the whole family system and those outside it.

- Workers should try to understand a family's patterns of communication before attempting to help the service user and carers to change the ways in which they interact with each other.

- Tasks completed between family meetings can provide material and/or opportunities to practise new skills to inform future meetings.

- Education in family work is as much about what the family workers learn, as it is about what the carers and service user gain.

- The service user is recognised and treated as the expert with regard to his or her experience of psychosis within the whole family work process.

- The educative process in family work is not synonymous with promoting the service user's insight with regard to psychosis.

- Carers' grief needs to be acknowledged and (possibly to avoid putting at risk the health of the carer) may sometimes have to become the focus for specific intervention before he or she can take part in effectively promoting the service user's recovery.

Recommended further reading

Barrowclough, C. and Tarrier, N. (1997) *Families of Schizophrenic Patients*. Cheltenham: Stanley Thornes.

Department of Health (1999) *National Service Framework for Mental Health: Modern Standards and Service Models*. London: The Stationery Office.

Kuipers, L., Leff, J. and Lam, D. (2002) *Family Work for Schizophrenia. A Practical Guide* (2nd edn). London: Gaskell.

Lafond, V. (1998) 'The Grief of Mental Illness: Context for the Cognitive of Therapy of Schizophrenia.' In C. Perris and P. McGorry (eds) *Cognitive Psychotherapy of Psychotic and Personality Disorders: Handbook of Theory and Practice.* Chichester: Wiley & Sons.

Lafond, V. (2002) *Grieving Mental Illness* (2nd edn). Toronto: University of Toronto Press.

Miller, W. and Rollnick, S. (2002) *Motivational Interviewing. Preparing People to Change Addictive Behaviour* (2nd edn). London: Guilford Press.

10

How to Promote Recovery Through Family Work

Focusing on recovery

Once you have established the structure for effective family meetings, and increased the family's understanding of the service user's psychosis, you can focus on working with them on their long-term goals. This will build on the spirit of optimism that you have fostered since your first meetings with family members, really helping everyone to work towards recovery.

It is important to recognise that recovering from psychosis does not equate to eradicating it. As we know, an acute psychotic episode brings with it the risk of further acute episodes, so recovery from psychosis needs to be considered within this context. However this does not mean there has to be a focus by mental health service providers and/or families on its potentially negative impact; indeed this can destroy the individual's attempts to overcome his or her difficulties (Chadwick 1997). Moreover, there are numerous positive personal accounts of individuals' recoveries from various mental illnesses, such as those recounted in Repper and Perkins' book *Social Inclusion and Recovery* (2003), which serve to remind us just how optimistic we should be.

The importance of promoting recovery is now recognised as being central to the role of all mental health workers in Britain through its inclusion as one of the 'Ten Essential Shared Capabilities' (DH 2004), where it is defined as:

> Working in partnership to provide care and treatment that enables service users and carers to tackle mental health problems with hope and optimism and to work towards a valued life-style within and beyond the limits of any mental health problem. (p.3)

So we can see that as family workers we are very well placed to fulfil this role, as we model and promote a number of skills and techniques that help carers and service users realise their potential.

Reframing

Reframing is a means by which a situation can be viewed in another way or a statement reworded to offer a possible new perspective. This alternative meaning can sometimes provide an opportunity to see things more clearly, and even if the reframe is rejected, it can prompt a discussion that develops all party's understanding. This is very useful in family meetings, particularly because it allows suggested reframes to be put forward tentatively with the expressed intention of trying to clarify the meaning of something.

It is most usual for a reframe to embrace a positive perspective, which may then dramatically change the implication of an action or comment. For example, a mother may speak very critically to her daughter (the service user) about her apparent laziness. Within a family meeting one of the co-workers could offer a suggestion that the criticism is possibly an attempt to motivate the service user. If this reframe is accepted it then opens a way forward to discuss alternative ways to try to offer encouragement without using critical comments. This can result in reduced levels of expressed emotion that may lead to a further improvement in the service user's symptoms of psychosis. A further example is given by Miklowitz and Goldstein (1997) regarding a situation in which the service user expresses shame at having to accept his or her diagnosis and fears that it will lead to various losses in life. In their example this conflicts with the carer's acceptance of the diagnosis, thus causing disputes. The service user's struggle could be reframed as part of a developing acceptance of the illness that is therefore healthy and understandable, so not actually in conflict with the carer's view but merely less advanced.

Reframing is an important tool for dealing with resistance (Miller and Rollnick 2002), as it is a means to offer an alternative point of view that avoids the risk of confrontation. This is extremely useful when an issue is causing distress to one family member while another is denying the problem exists and thus refuses to take part in trying to resolve it. A reframe that may be accepted by both parties provides an opportunity for considering a shared resolution.

When developing and using reframing techniques mental health workers need to be firmly rooted in the core conditions of therapeutic relationships (Rogers, cited in Rogers and Stevens 1967), because if the service user is not central to the intervention then reframing can become a tool of negative manipulation. This could then cause the worker to lose the trust of both service user and carers.

We feel that reframing is probably one of the most important skills that we promote with service users and carers through our family interventions. If practised and used regularly, reframing can become an attitude and a good habit that can help individuals notice a positive perspective with opportunities for bringing about useful changes. In Box 10.1 we have listed of some of the possibilities generated by well-intentioned reframing.

Box 10.1 Possibilities that may be created by reframing

Reframing may help individuals to:

- see an issue or situation more clearly
- develop or increase insight
- develop new perspectives and/or a new frame of reference
- question previously held assumptions and reject distorted perceptions
- make understandable what was previously puzzling.

How to reframe

Good reframing is underpinned by the use of **active listening skills** such as paraphrasing and reflecting. These allow you to acknowledge a comment and possibly check out the meaning and/or the intent of the individual who made the original remark. You may go on to ask the person to whom the comment was made what it meant to him or her. You are then in a position to offer a reframe in which you should try to use similar language to that used in the original statement so that the two may easily be compared. We also try to work to our rule that a reframe should be expressed in a single breath, as it is usually its immediacy that makes it effective and, if it is too long, the meaning is often lost.

Next, you (or your co-worker) can encourage those directly involved to discuss the difference in the meanings and intentions underlying the original remark and the reframe. Here we find that using humour and involving other members of the family often assists this process and helps individuals to practise rephrasing their statements to more clearly express themselves. Over time we hope to see families adopting this skill without prompting, using it to recognise their joint attempts to cope with the impact of psychosis and to support one another.

Reframing can often generate strong emotions as individuals openly acknowledge their caring intent and recognise the effects of previous misinterpretations and misjudgements. As within all our family interventions, working with these emotions is just as important as developing new skills and, as ever, your interpersonal skills will be as vital as your ability to use specific family work techniques. In some cases it may be necessary to go on to use a problem-solving structure to deal with some issues that emerge as you explore possible reframes and, in practice, you will often find that reframing helps you generate new solutions to a family's problems, demonstrating the value of promoting these skills together.

Problem solving

In the past it was frequently the case, as we discussed in Chapter 2 (What is Family Work for Psychosis?), that the service user's mental illness and the associated symptomatic behaviours were seen as indivisible from his or her personality. This approach often caused the service user to be blamed for the family's distress, which then increased the stress for all concerned. Conversely (as is also described in Chapter 2) family interventions are based on stress vulnerability models that understand the problems of psychosis to be multi-factorial and therefore require collaboration between a service user, carers and mental health workers.

There has also been a tradition that mental health workers try to solve service users' presenting problems. Family work differs from this rather paternalistic approach through its long-term aim for family members to become equipped with a structure that they can use to solve any problem in their everyday lives as it arises, enabling them to grow independent from mental health service providers. Seeing the service user and carers as individuals with strengths and resources, rather than as part of a problem (Mohr *et al.* 2000), is key to facilitating this change of approach and promoting the whole family's recovery.

Problem solving is a core component of family work for psychosis, being one of the main ways we help service users and carers to address their needs in a manageable way. Its aim is to help family members to develop creative solutions to the problems they are grappling with, in a way that generally avoids any behaviours that can cause tensions within their home environment. This is usually helped by the use of a structured approach to tackling problems and setting goals that all family members can recognise and take part in.

In our role as family workers we sometimes encounter family members who approach problem solving with a great deal of energy and very little structure. This may have worked well enough before the service user's onset of illness, but is not usually too helpful when the family has the added strain of coping with psychosis, when it can be hard to maintain a feeling of control and order. A good way that we have found to describe this unhelpful chaotic behaviour, without it sounding critical, is to liken it to the character of Tigger, which many people are familiar with from the stories about Winnie the Pooh by A. A. Milne. This fellow is notorious for bouncing into a situation and wreaking havoc, before bouncing off again – a habit that some may recognise in themselves or other members of their family. We discovered this hint in a useful problem-solving manual by Allen and Allen (1997), which employs Milne's characters throughout to demonstrate a number of problem-solving techniques and, at times, we suggest this book to families as a potential resource.

Promoting a structured problem-solving framework

It is part of our role as family workers to maximise all family members' ability to focus on whatever the particular problem under review may be, to work together to seek solutions and thereby minimise any unnecessary tensions. To achieve this we recommend the use of a simple structured framework, such as that advocated by Falloon and colleagues (1984), which has a very straightforward six-step approach that we find most carers and service users can quickly grasp and recognise its benefits.

Before offering a new framework it is worth asking a family whether they already use a structure (possibly adopted from a carer's workplace) and if so might consider using it instead of our suggestion. However, you need to make sure that it is not too complicated to be understood by any family member who is less cognitively able, including the service user if he or she is distracted by positive symptoms of psychosis. Nonetheless, in practice you may find that more than one model can be combined, as we have shown in Appendix 11, where we have used some prompts from Allen and Allen (1997) to provide clarifying questions that enhance the function of the structure proposed by Falloon and colleagues (1984). In order to help you to judge the utility of any problem-solving structure to be used within family work for psychosis we have listed in Box 10.2 the benefits it should confer.

Box 10.2 Benefits of a structured problem-solving framework within family work

The structured problem-solving framework should be able to:

- help the family deal with specific problems generated by the psychosis
- help to turn problems into needs and then into goals, thereby avoiding the risk of blame that may arise from seeing the service user or carer as the problem
- shift the emphasis of intervention away from family deficits to a focus on strengths and directions for positive change
- focus on specific issues, in order to identify objectives and plan small achievable tasks
- offers a means to recognise successful strategies.

Falloon and colleagues' (1984) six-step problem-solving approach
Within this approach it is important to focus on one problem at a time, and then to identify small steps that are measurable and achievable and that lead towards a solution that suits the whole family. In practice, you will find it often helps to reframe the problem statement as a goal so that you are working towards a positive outcome rather than trying to eradicate something.

The first step in this six-step process helps a family to define the problem they wish to work on. This sounds simple but it may actually take some time to properly explore the specific issue to ensure that everyone is in agreement. We stress the need to spend time on this stage as it is the foundation of problem solving, and it is often due to misunderstandings here that the latter steps of the approach become muddled.

Having agreed about what to work on, everyone is invited to contribute possible solutions that may achieve the desired outcome, regardless of how useful or outrageous they might be – in fact, the more creative solutions are often born out of the most extraordinary suggestions. The advantages and disadvantages of each one are then considered, allowing the most suitable solution to be chosen in terms of its applicability, while also taking into account the resources and needs of all concerned. Next, you agree who is doing what, how and when, still paying careful attention to the resources available. This leads on to testing out the best solution, which can be seen as an experiment that will be reviewed at another family meeting when you will look at what went well and what was not so successful, and explore how the latter can be avoided or minimised in future.

A lack of optimism is sometimes apparent during this process through comments that demonstrate the presence of high expressed emotion. You should manage these either by modelling or using reframing in a way that avoids using critical comments, hostility and/or emotional over-involvement. One of the advantages of co-working, as mentioned earlier, is that it can help to avoid the family workers being drawn into emotional issues, while addressing the balance of alliances within a family meeting.

A worked example of the six-step problem-solving framework
A commonly experienced (fairly simple) problem that we frequently see families struggling with is the aggravation caused by the service user not getting up in the morning at a time that is seen as reasonable to the carer. This usually seems to lead to the carer becoming increasingly upset by this behaviour, with the service user upset by the carer's reaction, and so a vicious circle evolves (see Burbach *et al.* 2007 for a detailed explanation). We have therefore chosen this issue to demonstrate Falloon and colleagues' (1984) six-step problem-solving framework in practice. (Within this example the service user has been referred

to as him and the carer as her to simplify the description, but we do not mean to infer this problem does not occur with female service users and/or male carers.)

STEP 1

The *problem* is that the service user gets up late every day, which irritates the carer with whom he is living. This problem can be reframed to give an outcome that can be worded in positive terms rather than stating what will not happen. Therefore the *goal* is that he will get up at a time that is seen as reasonable to both himself and the carer.

STEP 2

A number of possible solutions are then listed without discussion:

- carer to wake the service user by removing the bed covers
- carer to prompt service user to go to bed earlier
- service user to make an appointment with his care coordinator to further investigate why he finds it so difficult to get up in the morning
- service user to stop taking all medication that causes sedation
- carer to buy the service user an alarm clock
- carer to bring the service user a cup of tea when she tries to wake him
- carer to continue to nag the service user every morning
- carer to throw cold water over the service user if he does not respond to her verbal prompts.

STEP 3

Every potentially positive suggestion is then considered for its advantages and disadvantages. So taking the solution of the carer continuing to nag as an example, the *advantages* of the carer's nagging are:

- sometimes service user gets up before noon
- without nagging, service user does not get up until 3 pm.

However, the *disadvantages* of nagging include:

- it upsets the carer
- it annoys the service user
- it doesn't produce a regular time for him to wake up.

The most extreme or potentially destructive suggestions are then *modified* or *put on hold*. So from the list above those that we would probably wish to exclude are:

- carer to throw cold water over the service user
- carer to wake the service user by removing the bed covers.

STEP 4

It is then possible to choose the best solution by weighing up all the advantages and disadvantages; sometimes it may be that combining more than one solution is likely to gain the maximum benefit. So in this case the family chose:

- carer to buy the service user an alarm clock
- carer to bring the service user a cup of tea ten minutes after she hears the service user's alarm go off.

STEP 5

When a solution or selection of solutions has been made it is important to make a note of who is doing what, when and how, while not forgetting to include how any new material resources will be obtained. For example:

- carer will buy an alarm clock when shopping on Thursday, using money from the service user's incapacity benefit
- service user and carer to agree what time the alarm should be set for and at what time the carer should bring in a cup of tea.

At the same time as planning the strategy for solving the problem *a time should be set when progress will be reviewed*:

- review how this plan worked out at the next family meeting in two weeks' time.

STEP 6

Review the progress. Celebrate successes and, if necessary, examine what did not go so well, in order to repeat the same six-step framework to problem-solve any emergent obstacles.

Promoting wider networks

It is well recognised that the experience of psychosis is associated with stigma that often leads to both service users and carers finding themselves more socially isolated than they would have been had the psychosis not occurred. This isolation in itself adds to the burden for carers (Fadden *et al.* 1987) and service users (Repper and Perkins 2003). It is also known that more than 35 hours per week for carers and the service user spent in face-to-face contact with each other increases the service user's risk of psychotic relapse (Brown *et al.* 1972). For this reason, it is useful for family workers to help all family members consider how they may either re-establish or broaden their social networks to reduce social isolation and the risk of unnecessary tensions building up at home.

Service users and carers may make some social contacts by attending therapeutic activities organised by their local mental health service providers. Indeed these can be a safe first step for those who have lost their confidence as a result of the psychosis, by offering an opportunity to meet others who understand something about living with a mental illness in informal situations. The problem-solving structure may also play a part in helping a family member to plan how to join in and ask for any necessary support to make it manageable.

There are a number of psychological therapies and psychosocial interventions available for service users that are likely to complement family work. However, we feel it is beyond the scope of this manual to explore these, but those wishing to know more may find a series of case studies that describe the impact of many possible psychosocial interventions collected by Vellerman and colleagues (2007) a useful resource. There are also some alternative or additional ways to get support that we will briefly explain within the following subsections of this chapter.

Multi-family groups

William McFarlane (2000) designed an intervention called psycho-educational multi-family groups, which aims to combine the family interventions that reduce psychotic relapse rates by lowering levels of expressed emotion in the service user's home environment with a group experience to 'counter family isolation and stigma' (p.75). This intervention, which is described in detail by McFarlane (1994), has shown very promising results where it has been implemented and has obvious benefits in terms of pooling the knowledge and skills of a number of families coping with psychosis. However, in our catchment areas we have never been able to offer psycho-educational multi-family groups in practice because all the families referred to us and our local family work colleagues have opted for an intervention that includes only their own family members.

Voluntary organisations

Some carers and service users will have had contact with a voluntary agency such as SANE, **Rethink** or the Manic Depression Fellowship prior to coming into contact with statutory mental health services. If so, and it was a good experience, they are likely to maintain this contact alongside the help received from statutory services. Others may not have heard of any of these organisations prior to their involvement with statutory mental health services so may need to be given some details about what is available, both locally and nationally.

Some service users and/or carers will associate statutory mental health services with enforced treatment, such as when a service user in Britain has required admission to hospital under a section of the Mental Health Act 1983. Following this type of experience a family may not wish to remain in contact with statutory services after the acute episode of illness has been resolved. In such cases, ongoing input from a voluntary organisation could be recommended to try to ensure they do not suffer from a lack of information or support.

In some localities the local statutory service providers have limited resources to devote to anything other than managing acute mental health issues, so it is left to the voluntary services to deliver the longer-term recovery-orientated provision. Whatever your local situation, in your role as a family worker you will probably benefit from developing a good working relationship with the voluntary agencies offering support to carers within your area. This will both allow you to recommend services knowledgeably to those who might use them, as well as influence their continuing operation and development to meet the needs of any family members with whom you work. It has been our experience over many years of practice that voluntary agencies are often much more able to provide a flexible response to unusual family needs, and on numerous occasions we have appreciated their input at times when our own organisations have struggled to provide a solution.

Carer support groups

In has been known for decades that carers often feel isolated as a result of the experience of caring for someone with a severe mental illness (Creer and Wing 1974). Attendance of a carers' support group can help to normalise the experience of caring by providing access to a social network of people who understand what it is like living with someone who has psychotic experiences. These groups may offer practical support, suggestions for practical solutions to problems, advice on benefits and advocacy, and a whole range of information about mental illnesses and the available treatments.

Carer support groups also offer an opportunity for carers to express their sadness, fears and/or anger in a safe environment, as most carers worry that if they display these emotions at home they will upset the service user and risk interrupting his or her recovery. For this reason (in our experience) carers are reluctant to attend a group that is open to both service users and carers.

While we do not feel that, in the longer term, carers' groups should be run by mental health workers who are not carers themselves, it is often useful for one or two workers in a locality to help set up a new group or support a group that is failing to attract new members. Once a group is established it can then be helpful to those carers who run it to have access to a mental health worker within statutory services to provide a means to report concerns as well as an opportunity to debrief if necessary.

The timing and venue for a carers' group need to be chosen carefully as it appears that some carers prefer to come a group that allows them to keep their attendance private from the service user (Smith 2003). Therefore it is usually inappropriate to run a long-term support group from an in-patient ward. However, carers' need for comfort and information during a service user's in-patient treatment is well recognised (Mohr *et al.* 2000) so appropriate immediate individual support and guidance should be available there.

Advocacy and developing services

Some carers and service users are helped to come to terms with the experience of psychosis by becoming involved in improving mental health services for those who will use them in the future, gaining comfort from knowing they are making a difference (Smith 2003). There are numerous activities that they may become involved in, including sitting on planning committees, staff training, participating in the interview and selection process for new mental health workers and managers, as well as becoming mental health workers themselves in some cases.

As with most paid employment, taking on any of these roles is likely to bring with it some benefits in terms of social contact with other like-minded people, as well as many other facets of job satisfaction. However, it is vital that the ways to manage any fluctuations in the service user's health and care needs are incorporated into any such role and its responsibilities to avoid adding to family tensions rather than relieving them (Mistral *et al.* 2007).

Endings and booster sessions

Family work should always be introduced as a time-limited intervention, but this does not mean that it is possible to predict at the start of the process how many meetings will be offered overall. The essence of family work is to leave the family with skills that they can embrace and continue using when the workers no longer visit regularly. When this end has been achieved is something that needs to be negotiated between the carers, service user and family workers, recognising that an intervention that goes on too long could undermine family members' ability to develop confidence that they will be able to manage without the workers present, thereby creating an ongoing dependence.

While there is no defined time by which workers should disengage from a family there may be occasions when a family worker has to leave due to a change of job responsibilities or personal circumstances. In such a case the family should be given as much notice as possible, including some discussion about whether or not to introduce a new co-worker. It is also possible that some families may want to disengage before the workers feel the process is complete. Again this needs to be acknowledged without making the family feel guilty, to leave them with a means to make further contact with services should they want to re-engage (Kuipers *et al.* 2002).

When the ending is reached, feelings of loss (and possibly abandonment) may need to be explored. An ending is naturally the time to review individuals' learning and strengths, to look at the new resources that exist within the family and celebrate the achievements of all concerned. Some families may find it difficult to explore their achievements if the service user's psychotic symptoms have not improved as much as was hoped for. Others may struggle to openly discuss their successful achievements if they are still not really comfortable expressing praise for each other, so do not force it! However, as you will have worked on helping them to give one another positive as well as negative feedback, as described in Chapter 7 (How to Prepare for Family Work Meetings) this may not be an issue.

It is also important to prepare a family for possible setbacks, by explaining that this could happen and that it is normal. Here it may be useful to encourage them to use their reframing skills to enable them to recognise that a setback can be a good opportunity for further learning and thereby a point from which to move forward again. It may help some families to have a contact number that can be used should things get too difficult or if the ways in which they have been coping are no longer working. In such cases a single 'booster session' may be sufficient to reinforce their coping strategies, but for others a longer series of follow-up meetings may be necessary.

As yet the long-term effectiveness of family intervention has had little research attention, although we know its impact can still be noticed many years after the initial intervention was provided (Tarrier *et al.* 1994). Our local research (Drage *et al.* 2004) suggests that families do sometimes reach a point at which they feel ready for further family meetings to work together with facilitation to help them move on again, especially in cases where the service user's recovery is slow. We have also found the need for additional meetings when the service user has gained insights through individual interventions (that he or she wants to share, with help, with other family members) after the initial series of family meetings have ceased. If you have experience in this area we hope you will publish your findings to share your learning.

Finally, it is hoped that you will remember to appreciate your own efforts and those of your co-worker. With every family with whom you work you will probably have been on quite a journey yourself, and will benefit from taking time to reflect and process this experience, both with your co-worker and within supervision.

Evaluating family work

The first generation of family work studies measured the effectiveness of the interventions in terms of reducing the rates of schizophrenia relapse for service users (although what constituted a relapse was often not consistently defined) and, in particular, lessening the need for admission to hospital. Within most current mental health service configurations, however, with their increasing investment in crisis resolution and home treatment (DH 2001), this is no longer a fitting way to judge the impact of family work for psychosis.

You might suppose that reapplying some of the initial family work assessments would provide useful outcome measures in terms of a decreased score on the General Health Questionnaire (Goldberg and Williams 1988) or an increase on the Knowledge About Schizophrenia Interview (Barrowclough *et al.* 1997). We initially thought this, but found in practice that many carers score so highly on the KASI at the beginning of family work (despite lacking a clear picture of the service user's psychotic experience) that there is little scope to demonstrate an impact by this measure. And, as we have found that many carers are actually unwilling to complete the GHQ, this does not appear to be the right tool to judge the effectiveness of family work either. Moreover, neither of these tools is designed for the service user so we would capture only part of the family's views by these measures. For this reason, we have never adopted them as outcome measures in our routine practice.

As we feel it is hard to measure the effectiveness of family interventions through any currently available quantitative measures we are presently involved in research led by a carer (Drage *et al.* 2004; Mistral *et al.* 2007) to try to devise an appropriate, simple-to-use outcome measure. In the meantime, we have decided to include a number of testimonials, shown in Boxes 10.3–10.6, from people who have taken part (or continue to partake) in family work for psychosis, to hear from them how they evaluate the intervention.

Box 10.3 A father's personal reflection on the effectiveness of family work

To experience a psychotic storm first-hand must be a terrifying ordeal; to experience it twice, and again, and once more, must exhaust every adverb and adjective one can think of – that is, if thinking is at all possible. From the outside, the sufferer appears to change and change again, and becomes a gross, almost obscene distortion of what they once were both mentally and physically. If this sufferer is your son or daughter then you start believing in aliens. Every known reference point disappears, every once shared value turns upside down and a form of insanity creeps through the family structure like an ugly dangerous virus threatening every relationship, every hard-won and precious insight.

Two of our five children were struck down by psychosis; even the washing-up in the sink began to look menacing! I had taught about psychopathology for years, but this knowledge was something else and what I knew was no help. There was no help anywhere except hard-nosed indifferent professionals presiding over a hopeless acute ward bedlam. Or so it all seemed to me then.

Then I met a family worker from the Avon and Wiltshire Mental Health Partnership NHS Trust; a special kind of family worker. She needed to be! I got angry with her. I jumped up and down. I ranted and raved about despicable mental health services. I boasted about my knowledge. I gushed out what I would do if certain things were not done. I did my best to shock her. I wanted a big big row! Did she not know how much damage I could do? What did she know about the disgrace, the stigma, the pain, the grief, the embarrassment and the hopelessness that I felt?

She took it all – again and again. She stayed there and listened, and eventually she reflected back to me my poor mixed-up angry self until I began to melt inside; until I was able to tell my story to this person and see those things that I needed to see and do. Only then was I able to feel a glimmering of hope and realise what I could do to come alongside my wife and family and start to be some kind of anchor for them, even now, especially now.

Looking back on those days I do believe that this encounter was the turning point for me. The lady in question was superbly equipped for she knew what to do and what not to do, and how. This was 'beyond the manual' stuff and could only be offered by someone who had written it; she had. She remains a good personal friend and valued colleague.

Box 10.4 A mother's testimony to the effectiveness of family work for psychosis

Before the family workers stepped in to help we were as a family fragmenting. The trauma and feelings of deep loss left us with little sense of hope for a meaningful future for our son or for our marriage. So how did this intervention help? It helped to address my feelings of deep loss, guilt and isolation, as well as helping the family find practical solutions to some of our problems; this prevented further damage to our family, including my marriage.

The real sense of realistic hope that was engendered helped my husband and I to support our son, and subsequently our youngest daughter, in constructive ways, without becoming over-involved. We also learnt to work in partnership with professionals in general, as it is true to say that we remain the constant influence in our care for our son and daughter, while professionals tend to move on.

Without this intervention I believe that our son's road to recovery would have been much longer, possibly resulting in many more hospital admissions, and our daughter's care would have been somewhat inferior in quality. This intervention has also enabled me to help other carers by becoming a coordinator of a Rethink (severe mental illness) Carers' Support Group.

Box 10.5 A service user's comments on the impact of family work on his illness

The family work programme turned out to be a huge turning point in my battle against bipolar disorder. Before the family work, the illness had taken away my career, reduced my feelings of self-worth to rock bottom and put huge strain on my marital relationship. I was left caught in cycle of frequent mood swings, which were taking away my will to live.

Family work tackled this on a number of levels; first, it gave us both a huge morale boost, simply by giving us something positive around which to focus our energies rather than continuing to be left to flounder. Second, it rebuilt trust and communication between my wife and I, which allowed us to start working together again, rather than being in near permanent conflict. Third, it provided a framework around which we could work together on improving my health, rather than simply fire-fighting against individual mood swings. Finally, achieving success in this work, and seeing my health improve as a result, helped rebuild my feelings of self-worth.

At the end of the family work programme my health, relationship and feelings of self-worth had all improved beyond recognition. We also had a set of tools and techniques, which we have been able to use since the family work to continually improve all these three areas. Even with the family work our battle against my illness was a tremendous struggle, but it was a struggle we were able to overcome, rather than one we could not. Since I completed the family work I have had only one mood swing in nearly three years, despite taking no regular medication, and we managed to get through that 'high' together without the need for any professional support.

The key word is 'family', as I could not have beaten this on my own and my wife could not have continued to help me without the support and new direction provided by the family work.

Box 10.6 A mother's journey

Watching someone's mind unravel and fall apart is a very traumatic experience, especially when it is someone you love. Our family suffered for nearly four years when a son/brother became psychotic. It is a very lonely and frightening experience. We sought help through the usual channels of primary and secondary care, but our efforts did not provide the help we had expected, either to him or to ourselves. There was little benefit from the three in-patient admissions and we seemed to encounter professionals who kept us at arm's length and regarded us as hostile and interfering. No one prepares you for the feelings of shock, horror, guilt, anger and helplessness when this happens, and no one came forward to offer us support or the glimmer of hope that life could improve.

When the words 'family intervention' were mentioned as I was leaving an in-patient unit one evening I felt that at last someone was thinking about all of us who were suffering as a result of the illness. I had no idea what the words implied, but it felt like this could be the start of something better for the whole family. Although at times a difficult process for all of us, it helped us to confront the illness openly, to share things that were problems for all of us, to look for solutions together and, above all, to have hope for a better future. The start of a recovery process.

This has indeed been the case. There have been no admissions to hospital for six years and our son now lives independently. There have been setbacks and times when the illness has threatened to close in and overwhelm us, but we are stronger, more vigilant and better equipped to stop it from engulfing us and causing severe relapse. I have been supported and encouraged by a professional with an extraordinary capacity to understand the family's neglected and undervalued position in someone's journey through mental illness; this has given me the desire and opportunity to develop an information pack for families and friends of someone suffering mental distress. This in turn has given me the opportunity to work with staff at local and national levels to understand the benefits of including family members not only in the planning of an individual's care, but also in planning service delivery and design.

We continue to benefit from this service and we continue our journey of recovery.

Summary

A problem-solving structure can help service users and carers pool their resources so that it is possible for them to work effectively together towards their individual and collective goals. If family members do not already possess the necessary communication skills, using a structured framework is likely to both identify the deficiencies and provide a forum to learn and practise any necessary new skills.

Reframing is a technique for looking at a phrase or action from a new angle. It usually offers a positive perspective and, even if the reframe is ultimately rejected, the debate it provokes will almost always generate new understandings for all concerned. Most service users and carers will be helped by learning reframing skills and a problem-solving structure, which tend to complement each other and help family members work together towards their individual and shared goals.

The way that the process of family work draws to an end is important, and if it is a brutal or unsatisfactory experience it can negate much of what was gained through family intervention. Therefore carers, service users and family workers should try to come to a realistic agreement with regard to what the end point should be, and how, having reached it, it will be recognised. This will most probably relate to the needs assessed at the beginning of the process than be defined by a set number of family meetings. Whenever this ending occurs most families will benefit from knowing that they can meet the co-workers again for one or more follow-up meetings should the need arise.

Key points

- Developing shared coping strategies and problem-solving skills requires good communication skills, which service users and carers can learn together through family work if they do not already have them at the start of the family intervention.

- Effective collective problem solving by carers and the service user is facilitated by the use of a shared structured framework.

- Obstacles encountered when working through a structured problem-solving framework can sometimes generate an understanding of where communication skills need to be enhanced in a way that family members find acceptable.

- If families have developed coping strategies that work for them (even if these appear somewhat unusual to the mental health service providers) family workers should never try to enforce any changes.

- Reframing is a non-confrontational means to proffer an alternative meaning for a situation or statement; even if the reframe is not accepted the discussion it promotes usually creates new understandings.

- How the pattern of regular family meetings ends is as important as how the intervention begins. Service users and carers report that they welcome an opportunity for ad hoc 'booster sessions' after the end of the formal family work process, to reinforce their coping strategies.

- Some carers will find that their sense of coping with psychosis in their own family is enhanced by going on to provide support to other carers and/or becoming involved in improving mental health services. Family workers are well placed to identify carers who may take on such roles, and to offer them support and encouragement.

Recommended further reading

Allen, R. and Allen, S. (1997) *Winnie the Pooh on Problem Solving.* London: Methuen.

Chadwick, P. (1997) *Schizophrenia: The Positive Perspective.* London: Routledge.

Department of Health (1999) *National Service Framework for Mental Health: Modern Standards and Service Models.* London: The Stationery Office.

Falloon, I., Boyd, J. and McGill, C. (1984) *Family Care of Schizophrenia.* New York: Guildford Press.

Miklowitz, D. and Goldstein, M. (1997) *Bipolar Disorder. A Family-Focused Treatment Approach.* London: Guilford Press.

Miller, W. and Rollnick, S. (2002) *Motivational Interviewing. Preparing People to Change Addictive Behaviour* (2nd edn). London: Guilford Press.

Repper, J. and Perkins, R. (1996) *Working Alongside People with Long Term Mental Health Problems.* London: Chapman & Hall.

Repper, J. and Perkins, R. (2003) *Social Inclusion and Recovery.* Edinburgh: Bailliere Tindall.

Appendices

We offer the documents contained within these appendices for you to use freely in your work with families, without any copyright restrictions. We do this because we wish the spread of family work for psychosis to be as rapid as possible, to play our part in overcoming some of the barriers we know to exist. Our practice has benefited from the generosity of others, most notably Ian Hughes, who shared his paperwork with us in 1998 when he led STEP (the Serious mental illness Therapeutic and Educational Project) in Cardiff. Nonetheless, there are scores of others too numerous to mention by name; we hope you will recognise yourselves and celebrate your contribution.

We want to maintain this trend of generosity among family workers, so that between us we try to support all families coping with psychosis. All we ask is that you share your developments with us: if you have suggestions for how any of our paperwork may be improved please let us know so that the families we work with directly and indirectly (through our teaching and supervisory roles) may benefit.

Glossary of terms

Active Listening Skills – skills used to develop an understanding about what the person is saying and meaning, also to help the person know that you are listening to them. Such skills include:

- reflecting
- summarising
- paraphrasing
- accurate empathy
- the use of open questions, which require more than 'yes' or 'no' as an answer.

Ambient stress – the usual day to day background stress experienced from home, work, leisure and/or social activities.

Atypical antipsychotic medication – newer forms of medication used to treat psychosis by primarily blocking dopamine and some of the serotonin receptors in the brain. They are more targeted towards certain receptors in the brain so generally have fewer side effects than *typical antipsychotic medication*. Within therapeutic doses they should not cause movement disorders.

Belief system – a set of particular views held that are not necessarily backed up by conclusive evidence. These beliefs may be accepted by a society, group or individual.

Causal attributions – the reasons that people give for why things happen.

Circular causality – the relationship between cause and effect is interrelated in a circular fashion; therefore, there is no single cause that can be blamed.

Clinical governance – the act of governing or controlling practice(s) within a health service in order to promote the delivery of safe and effective interventions, by identifying benchmarks of good practice against which services can be judged.

Collusion – the act of opting into a secret understanding with one or more individuals in a way that excludes others.

Demographic – relates to the births, deaths and other statistics of those involved.

Enmeshed – tangled up together, not able to define the boundary between each other; this term is often used by systemic family therapists to describe very close family relationships.

Estranged – caused to feel less close; this term is often used by systemic family therapists to describe a distant family relationship.

Face validity – clearly conveys a meaning that is easily understood by many people.

Family system – from systems theory; a fundamental system of kinship, the first group that a person usually has experience of.

Genogram – a diagrammatic representation of past and present family members and their relationships to each other.

Ground rules – basic rules agreed to regulate action and facilitate cooperation between members of a group of people that come together for a particular purpose.

Homeostasis – a state of balance or equilibrium maintained within a system.

Informal carers – friends, relatives or acquaintances that offer support and care to a person without being paid to do so.

Integrate – bring together different parts to make a whole. The whole is greater than the sum of its parts while the part is greater than its role in the whole. When models are integrated they combine to such an extent that you can no longer clearly identify the component parts unless you deconstruct the model. It differs from an eclectic approach, in which the component parts remain isolated and are used separately so the component parts remain unaltered. This can be exemplified using a food analogy of the difference between a curry, with its integrated ingredients, and the separate items in the traditional British meal of roast beef and Yorkshire pudding.

Inter-rater reliability – ensures that, regardless of who is completing a particular assessment, a similar result or score will be reached.

Join/joining – the act of linking together to support in an activity; to work collaboratively.

Likert scale – an attitude scale using ratings from a large number of statements in which respondents select and grade their responses from strongly agree though to strongly disagree. Scoring is calibrated positively and negatively (according to the statements) then summed to produce a total score. Named after Rensis Likert (1903-81) an American sociologist and economist.

Negative symptoms – an absence or reduction in a person's usual characteristics, such as loss of interest or ability to get pleasure from certain situations, loss of social contacts, fewer thoughts, limited conversation, loss of attention, lack of motivation and lack of emotions.

Neuroleptic medication – refers to the medication's action of wrapping around the nerve to treat psychotic illness, rather than an antidepressant to treat depression. Traditionally affected the four pathways for dopamine, a neurotransmitter that is able to transport a message through the nerve pathways, thus reducing the amount of dopamine there. Most commonly now referred to as antipsychotic medication (see *atypical antipsychotic medication*). However, there is some question as to whether this is an accurate description, as this type of medication is not always 100 per cent effective in being able to eradicate psychosis.

Oculogyric crisis – occurs as a side effect of neuroleptic drug treatment. Initial symptoms are a fixed stare and may be combined with restlessness and agitation, followed by maximal upward sustained deviation of the eyes which is often very painful. It can develop into a recurrent syndrome brought on by stress and/or medications such as neuroleptics, lithium, carbamazepine, benzodiazepines and even the influenza vaccine.

Pathogenic – causing illness.

Phenomenological – an exploration of a person's experiences as opposed to trying to assess an objective reality.

Positive symptoms – symptoms that are additional to the person's usual experience, such as hearing voices or holding unusual beliefs.

Prodrome – non-specific symptom that is noticed before the symptoms of a particular illness are apparent, and which indicates the impending risk of illness. A psychotic prodrome may include subtle changes in behaviour, affect or thoughts that, if left unmanaged and/or untreated, are very likely to progress to a full psychotic episode.

Psychological transitions – movement from one place to another or one state to another.

Qualitative – a research term concerned with describing the meaning of words rather than the statistical analysis of numerical data.

Reframe/reframed – acknowledges the validity of the person's observations, but offers a new meaning or interpretation for them. In this way the information is recast into a new perspective.

Reliability – a term ascribed to an assessment tool or measure that gives the same result time after time if used in the same situation.

Rethink – the largest severe mental illness charity in the UK, formerly known as the *National Schizophrenia Fellowship*.

Schema – a cognitive framework constructed by an individual, which encompasses ideas and concepts in a way that enables him or her to take action in particular situations. The word schema is often used to describe an absolute core belief about the world, others and oneself.

Semi-structured interviews – interviews used in research or clinical practice that do not give detailed and specific instructions for use but provide useful prompts and a framework that guide a conversation to try to ensure that it covers the topics of interest to the interviewer.

Sensitive – to be affected by changes and quick to detect and/or respond. When the term is used in relation to an assessment tool, it refers to the tool's ability to detect a change or response in the area of interest.

Significant other – refers to the person who is identified as most closely involved in the person's care; they may not be legally married, related or next of kin.

Signs and symptoms – the features that indicate (or are suggestive of) a particular illness or condition.

Socratic questioning – a specific technique used to elicit answers from questions within a dialogue, to reveal inconsistencies in accepted opinions.

Statistically significant – the degree to which a result has not occurred by chance but is due to the intervention under examination. This significance will be noted as a probability, which may be anywhere between 1 (an absolute certainty) to 0 (denoting an absolute impossibility). For example, when $p=0.08$ this means that the result could only have happened by chance in less than 8 per cent of the cases (8 in 100). The smaller the p value the more significant it is statistically, meaning the more confident we can be that an outcome did not just happen by chance.

Stress – pressure or tension exerted on a person (or object), which can have a positive or negative effect. A negative effect can create a mental or emotional strain and have physical consequences.

Supervisee – a person who is in receipt of supervision.

Thematic analysis – a process to analyse and interpret qualitative research data, drawing single items under overarching themes that describe their meaning.

Therapeutic alliance – a relationship in which two or more people agree to form an alliance and work together even when there are challenges and struggles.

Thorn Diploma – a degree-level course to develop the skills and knowledge needed to work effectively with those who experience psychosis. Originally, Sir Jules Thorn funded its development, hence its name. It consists of modules that relate to individual and family work.

Typical antipsychotic medication – older forms of medication used to treat psychosis by blocking dopamine receptors in the brain, less specific and generally affecting more receptors in the brain than the newer ones so therefore have a wider range of side effects than *atypical antipsychotic medication.*

Validated – having gone through a validation procedure before being used.

Validity – the degree to which a test measures what it sets out to.

Vulnerability – tendency to come to harm; a likelihood that an illness or condition may develop.

Who is a carer?

A carer is a person who gives up their own time, often without payment, recognition or thanks, to help another person who is disadvantaged due to physical or mental illness or disability. They may be expected to be available 24 hours a day, 365 days a year. Without training they may be expected to act as a nurse, companion, taxi driver and financial adviser.

Carers are, in fact, normal people who, out of a sense of love, duty and compassion, struggle to live their own lives and, at the same time, do their best to help a spouse, sibling, offspring or friend to achieve something in their lives. This carer may be the only person who is trusted by the unwell friend or relative.

Carers ask only to be given guidance, information and a little time to understand and learn how to cope with a situation that, if they did not deal with, would be a burden on the community in both time and money. They recognise the role of professionals in the various disciplines and appreciate the pressure that they work under. Carers ask that their expertise is also recognised and that workers talk to them and keep them informed of what is happening.

This definition comes from the Carers' Information Pack produced by the Avon and Wiltshire Mental Health Partnership NHS Trust. The information found in this pack is designed to assist the carer in accessing information that will help to fulfil the role in the best way. It has been written by a carer, for carers – as she says, 'by someone who knows what it is like. The fact that this pack exists will help carers access information out of normal working hours and is seen as a godsend to a carer in desperation'.

Copies of this carers' pack can be downloaded free of charge from:

www.carershelpcarers.org.uk

If you would like to find out how this pack was developed and funded, or if you require any further information, please contact Gina Smith on 01225 383653.

Family Work for Psychosis

We know that families can do a great deal to help their relative recover from a psychotic episode. We aim to support families in this process by sharing information and ways of working, to help you to improve the things you can, and accept the things you cannot change.

How can you find out more about family work?
This may be from your GP, or care coordinator, through a leaflet, a friend, voluntary agency or some other source.

↓

How do you and your family get referred for family work?
This could be by your care coordinator or another family member.

↓

What happens at the first meeting for you and your family with the family workers?
This provides an opportunity to get to discuss the needs of the family and how this service could help. You will also be given a copy of the *Commitment to Carers* booklet.

↓

Do you all get a chance to put your views across?
Each family member is offered a private meeting to discuss how psychosis affects their life. Workers will help you look at how you cope day to day, the resources you have, including your knowledge about the illness, medication and other possible treatments such as cognitive behaviour therapy.

↓

What happens in the first family work session?
This carries on from your initial meeting, to continue to assess the situation, to identify problems, what you do that works and where you need help.

↓

What happens in the following sessions?
The work continues, building on the family's skills and knowledge, helping you to feel more able to cope and manage problems.
To start with, sessions for all family members to attend will usually take place fortnightly, tailing off gradually in step with the family's confidence.

↓

How does the work end?
You and your family workers will agree when there is no longer a need to meet regularly. They will probably leave you with a contact number so that you can ask for further help if the need arises.

Family Work Leaflet

FAMILY WORK FOR PSYCHOSIS

Avon and Wiltshire
Mental Health Partnership NHS Trust

Providing additional help to families to enable them to help, more effectively, family members who suffer from psychosis.

WHAT IS THE PROBLEM?

Psychosis is a common mental illness that can affect more than one in every hundred in the population.

Illness often appears during late adolescence or early adulthood, at a time of life that is full of hopes and expectation. The disruption of plans caused by the illness can add a great deal to the burden of the illness, both for the sufferer and their family.

While professional help is certainly needed, the family can also make a great difference if they know how to help.

WHAT CAN HELP?

It has been shown that work, with the sufferer and his or her family, can reduce the risk of becoming unwell again and improve the quality of life for those concerned. Professionals call this work 'psychosocial intervention' but in practice it just means that help is given to the whole family to improve their ability and confidence in tackling problems effectively, as well as information being offered about the illness itself and the services available, both locally and nationally.

HOW OUR SERVICE WORKS

People are usually referred to this service by the sufferer's care coordinator but the initial discussion about family work may be started by any of the family or professionals involved. Following referral, it is usual for two workers to contact the family to arrange an initial, informal meeting to discuss in more detail what the work entails and answer any questions. This meeting lasts for about an hour and can take place in the family home, in hospital or at the community mental health team base. From this, any future work to help the family can be planned.

OTHER USEFUL SERVICES

Mind
Granta House
15–17 Broadway
London E15 4BQ
0845 766 0163
website: www.mind.org.uk

Manic Depression Fellowship (MDF)
Castle Works
21 St Georges Road
London SE1 6ES
0845 634 0540
website: www.mdf.org.uk

Samaritans
08457 909090
website: www.samaritans.org.uk

Saneline
0845 767 8000
website: www.sane.org.uk

Rethink
28 Castle Street
Kingston-upon-Thames
Surrey KT1 1SS
0845 456 0455
website: www.rethink.org

Leaflets containing more information regarding these services are available from GP surgeries.

FOR MORE INFORMATION CONTACT:

Gina Smith (Beacon Award Winner 1999)
Consultant Nurse
Family Work Service, Room 7.25
University of Bath, Wessex House
Bath BA2 7AY

Telephone: 01225 323653

Or contact your local family work service coordinator: [Name]

Who Can Help Me?

At the Hospital

The named nurse for . . . .

is: . . . . You can speak to him/her to answer
any questions or talk about your concerns.

On ward: . . . .

Telephone number: . . . .

Visiting times: . . . .

Ward rounds: . . . .

Consultant/doctor: . . . .

Ward manager/modern matron: . . . .

In the community

Other carers you can talk to: . . . .

. . . .

Your local support group is: . . . .

. . . .

Address: . . . .

. . . .

The date of the next meeting is: . . . .

Assessment of Carer's
Needs Initial Assessment/Review*

*Please delete as necessary

Name of carer. . . . .

Name of person
you care for . . . .

Hosp no: . . . .

D.O.B.: . . . .

Carer's D.O.B.: . . . .

Carer's ethnic origin: . . . .

Do you think of yourself as a carer? Yes ☐   No ☐

What do you do for the person you care for?

. . . .

. . . .

Do you know how this is reflected in the Care Plan? . . . .

. . . .

. . . .

Do you have a copy of the Care Plan? Yes ☐   No ☐

Does your role put pressure on you: e.g. work, financially, with other family members?

. . . .

. . . .

What information or support might help you to manage your role better?

. . . .

. . . .

Is there anything you would like to change about your role as a carer, if other services could be put in place?

. . . .

. . . .

. . . .

Do you know what to do if you feel unsafe or unable to cope?

. . . .

. . . .

Other information it may be useful for us to know?

. . . .

. . . .

. . . .

. . . .

Is a more detailed assessment required? Yes ☐ No ☐

Is this needed urgently? Yes ☐ No ☐

How often would you like your situation reviewed?

Monthly   Quarterly   6 Monthly   Annually

Name of carer . . . .

Signature . . . .   Date . . . .

Name of assessor . . . .

Signature . . . .   Date . . . .

Name of care coordinator (*if different*) . . . .

Signature . . . .   Date . . . .

Give a copy of this Carer's Assessment/Review to the carer and keep one in carer section of case notes

Family Work Referral Form

Referred by . . . .   Care coordinator. . . . .

Date. . . . .   Medical consultant. . . . .

Where is the service user currently residing?

Name. . . . .   Marital Status . . . .

Address . . . .   Date of Birth . . . .

Telephone number . . . .   Members of Household. . . . .

Long-term aims and/or reason for referral:

Key professionals involved:

Is there a ward conference, CPA or other suitable forum for a family worker to discuss the case? If so, please give the date and time:

Is the service user aware of this referral?   Yes ☐   No ☐
Is the care coordinator aware of this referral?   Yes ☐   No ☐
Are there any risk factors to be taken into account?   Yes ☐   No ☐

Please return to: [Add name of Family Work Champion or whoever has local responsibility for allocating families to family workers]

Family Work
Skills Checklist (FWSC)

Name. . . . .   Date . . . .

A. Technical skill checklist:

Diagnosis

   1.   Explore knowledge of diagnosis

   2.   Explore feelings about the diagnosis

   3.   Emphasise how the family can help

Contents

   1.   Use client as case in point

   2.   Emphasise key areas of ignorance

   3.   Encourage discussion/experience

   4.   Encourage asking questions

Communication

   1.   Encourage listening to everyone, especially client

   2.   Emphasise turn-taking

   3.   Encourage sharing of feelings

   4.   Encourage each (especially quiet) member to actively participate

Main concerns

   1.   Explore main concerns

   2.   Get agreement

   3.   Get agreement on priority

   4.   Acknowledge individuals' concerns

   5.   Review past and present coping strategies

Agreeing on tasks

1. Specify in detail what the problem(s) is/are
2. Elicit possible solutions
3. Look at pros and cons of a possible solution
4. Compromise and agree on a desirable solution

Assigning tasks

1. Get everyone's agreement on a realistic task
2. Spell out the HOW, WHEN and WHAT to do in detail
3. Anticipate any problems
4. Express an interest to find out how the task goes in the next session

Reviewing success

1. Encourage family to see progress in small steps
2. Encourage positive reinforcement to each other
3. Build on success towards final goals
4. Reinforce good coping strategies

Reviewing failures

1. Find out *exactly* what happened
2. Get everyone's perspective on the issue
3. Therapist absolves the blame
4. Explore alternatives for less adaptive coping behaviour

Resetting tasks

1. Reset task, taking into account the reasons for the failure
2. Spell out the HOW, WHEN and WHAT to do in detail
3. Anticipate any further problems
4. Emphasis on review, in next session

B. Competence scale checklist

Interpersonal skill

1. Genuine, open, sincere; no role play

2. Warmth, concern

3. Professional – imposing structure and directive to a point

4. Relaxed confidence; competent and convincing in expressing an alternative point of view

5. Not critical, cold or hostile

6. Not patronising, condescending, ridiculing, or evasive of family questions

Understanding

1. Sensitive to and recognises feelings through what is said and conveyed implicitly

2. Therapist reflects back feelings

3. Shows understanding, by rephrasing and summarising what is said

4. Tone of voice should convey sympathetic understanding of family point of view, although family must remain objective

5. Grasps main points including any subtle connotations of anything else that may be going on; not too literal or tangential

6. Does not project own or conventional attitudes

Negotiating style

1. Attempted to get family agreement on issues

2. Invited elaboration, feedback and collaboration

3. Expressed views of family experiences and circumstances as tentative rather than dogmatic statements

4. Accepted family views as possible alternatives and, where possible, explored them

5. Open to correction and accepted it appropriately

6. Maintained an open and flexible style that respected the family, co-therapist and own position

Controlling the session

1. Ensured a general focus in and throughout the session

2. Limited irrelevant topics

3. If no progress was being made, interrupted and approached the issue from another perspective

4. Rescheduled any unfinished business

5. Skilful in directing family members to focus in depth on issues

6. Facilitated family members to speak to each other directly

Co-therapy skill

1. Evidence of task preparation

2. Evidence of sharing the task during the session

3. Elaboration of each other's statements

4. Modelled conflict resolution

5. Balanced alliances with individual family members

6. No hostility or criticism of each other (explicit or implicit)

Handling (expressed) emotion

1. Facilitated the airing of emotion

2. Listened and acknowledged the emotions

3. Normalised and diffused the emotions by removing blame

4. Sufficient time was spent dealing with emotions as they came up

5. Addressed areas (emotional) of special concern

6. Took some appropriate action aimed at long-term behavioural or attitudinal change

Feedback

1. Check that family understands therapist's concept of problems and/or interventions by summaries and writing down

2. Therapist to check she/he has understood family by giving a summary and asking the family to fine-tune

3. Ask family for feedback explicitly

4. Specifically ask for any negative feedback

5. Ask family for choice re course of action

6. Evaluation of session

Agenda

1. Introduce self and co-therapist and (briefly) explain roles

2. Set agenda together of problems and issues to focus on during session

3. Prioritise items

4. Adherence to the agenda

5. Not too slow in time pacing

6. Not too quick, and not switching or interrupting unnecessarily

Overall comments:

Family Work
Assessment (FWA) Form

Name: .... Date: ....

1. **Structure of family**

2. **History of problem (family's shared perspective)**

3. **Current symptoms and/or concerns**

4. **Typical day (daily activities/social contacts)**

5. **Admissions/medication/treatment (including attendance at day centres, etc.)**

6. **Service user's strengths, resources, coping strategies**

7. **Carer's strengths, resources, coping stategies**

8. **Service user's expectations of family intervention and current family needs**

9. **Carer's expectations of family intervention and current needs**

10. **Goals of intervention (If intervention not offered or accepted, specify why. Include the options given to the various family members)**

Family Meeting Notes

Service user's name: . . . .   Date and session number:. . . . .

People attending, in order of seating arrangement:

Objectives (to be agreed between co-therapists before meeting):

Agenda:

Comments on the content of the meeting:

Comments on family interactions and alliances between individuals:

Outcome of the visit, including a summary of progress to date if appropriate:

Goals for next meeting:

Actions to be taken and homework tasks to be completed before the next meeting:

Other comments (phone calls, contacts with other professionals, etc.):

Date of next meeting: . . . .   Time of next meeting: . . . .

Place of next meeting: . . . .

Signatures: . . . .

Solving Problems
and Achieving Goals

STEP 1: What is the problem or goal?

Talk about the problem or goal; listen carefully; ask questions; get everyone's opinion. Then write down *exactly* what the problem or goal is.

- This may be an active choice, usually in an effort to improve or make something better, or a passive one that is presented for solving by someone else or fate, such as the illness.

- Consider whether there are emotional factors involved. Sometimes the problem or situation does, and sometimes the individuals involved will have emotional associations either with the problem or with others who are involved. You can't always do much except be aware they are there, to ensure they do not influence you unduly.

- Once you have agreed what the problem is, try to organise your thoughts further. Consider where things are now, where you would like them to be – which would be your goal – and notice anything that may be in the way of your achieving the goal.

- It is particularly useful to consider in detail:

    - WHY should this problem be solved?

    - WHAT is the problem?

    - WHY is it a problem?

    - WHERE does the problem occur?

    - WHY does it occur there?

    - WHEN does the problem occur?

    - WHY does it occur then?

    - WHO is involved with the problem?

    - WHY are they involved?

    - HOW does the problem arise?

    - WHY does it arise in that way?

- Clarification at this stage will ensure that you are working on the right problem, and will prevent difficulties later in the process.

STEP 2: List all possible solutions

Put down *all* ideas, even bad ones. Get everybody to come up with at least one possible solution. List the solutions *without discussion* at this stage.

- Creativity and experience are both important when looking for possible solutions.
- Many people consider that they are not creative, but if family workers ensure a lack of judgement at this stage, the chances of imaginative suggestions being offered will be increased.
- Experience is just the remembering of having solved other problems in the past and not forgetting the things that worked, and also those that didn't.
- Every idea is important, because it leads to the next idea, even if it doesn't solve the problem directly.

STEP 3: Discuss each possible solution

Quickly go down the list of possible solutions and discuss the *main* advantages and disadvantages of each one.

STEP 4: Choose the 'best' solution

Choose the solution that can be carried out most easily to solve the problem.

- It is worth spending a little time here, refining the best solution to improve its chance of success. Try to think of all the possibilities.

STEP 5: Plan how to carry out the best solution

Consider the resources needed and likely major pitfalls. Practise difficult steps. Set time for review.

- This stage is about developing an action plan, creating a path from here to there.
- The plan lists all the things you need to get or do to put the chosen solution into action.
- In some cases, with large or complex problems, it may be advisable to try them out in a small way, to see if they work, before committing yourself completely. That way, if things don't work out exactly as you thought, you have a chance to alter them or modify them before using it in a big way.

STEP 6: Review implementation and praise *all* efforts

Focus on *achievement first.* Review plan. Revise as necessary.

Remember what the goal was so you can be sure how to define success. You may need to select criteria to measure the results of the solution.

References

Adams, J. and Scott, J. (2000) 'Predicting Medication Adherence in Severe Mental Disorders.' *Acta Psychiatrica Scandinavia 101*, 119–124.

Addington, J. and Burnett, P. (2004) 'Working with Families in Early Stages of Psychosis.' In J. Gleeson and P. McGorry (eds) *Psychological Interventions in Early Psychosis. A Treatment Handbook.* Chichester: Wiley.

Allen, R. and Allen, S. (1997) *Winnie the Pooh on Problem Solving.* London: Methuen.

Andreason, N. (1984) *The Broken Brain: The Biological Revolution in Psychiatry.* New York: Harper and Row.

Angermeyer, M. and Matschinger, H. (1996) 'Relatives' Beliefs about the Causes of Schizophrenia. *Acta Psychiatrica Scandinavica 93*, 199–204.

Atkinson, J. (1994) 'Grieving and Loss in Parents with a Schizophrenic Child.' *American Journal of Psychiatry 151*, 8, 1137–1139.

Attwood, M., Pedler, M., Pritchard, S. and Wilkinson, D. (2003) *Leading Change: A Guide to Whole Systems Working.* Bristol: The Policy Press.

Baguley, I., Butterworth, A., Fahy, K., Haddock, G., Lancashire, S. and Tarrier, N. (2000) 'Bringing into Clinical Practice Skills Shown to be Effective in Research Settings. A Follow-up of Thorn Training in Psychosocial Interventions for Psychosis.' In B. Martindale, A. Bateman, M. Crowe and F. Margison (eds) *Psychosis – Psychological Approaches and their Effectiveness.* London: Gaskell.

Bainbridge, M. (2002) 'Carers are People Too.' *Mental Health Today*, June, 24–27.

Barrowclough, C. and Tarrier, N. (1997) *Families of Schizophrenic Patients. Cognitive Behavioural Intervention.* Cheltenham: Stanley Thornes.

Barrowclough, C., Johnson, M. and Tarrier, N. (1994) 'Attributions, Expressed Emotion and Patient Relapse: An Attributional Model of Relatives' Response to Schizophrenic Illness.' *Behaviour Therapy 25*, 67–88.

Barrowclough, C., Tarrier, N. and Johnson, M. (1996) 'Distress, Expressed Emotion and Attributions in Relatives of Schizophrenia Patients.' *Schizophrenia Bulletin 22*, 4, 691–702.

Barrowclough, C., Tarrier, N., Watts, S., Vaughn, C., Bamrah, J. and Freeman, H. (1987) 'Assessing the Functional Value of Relatives' Knowledge about Schizophrenia.' *British Journal of Psychiatry 151*, 1–8.

Bateson, G., Jackson, D., Haley, J. and Weakland, J. (1956) 'Towards a Theory of Schizophrenia.' *Behavioral Science 1*, 251–264.

Bebbington, P. and Kuipers, L. (1994) 'The Predictive Utility of Expressed Emotion in Schizophrenia: An Aggregate Analysis.' *Psychological Medicine 24*, 707–718.

Becker, M. and Maiman, L. (1975) 'Sociobehavioral Determinants of Compliance with Health and Medical Care Recommendations.' *Medical Care 13*, 10–24.

Birchwood, B., Smith, J., Cochrane, R., Wetton, S. and Copestake, S. (1990) 'The Social Functioning Scale; The Development and Validation of a New Scale of Social Adjustment for use in Family Intervention Programmes with Schizophrenic Patients.' *British Journal of Psychiatry 157*, 853–859.

Birchwood, M. (2000) 'The Critical Period for Early Intervention.' In M. Birchwood, D. Fowler and C. Jackson (eds) *Early Intervention in Psychosis: A Guide to Concepts, Evidence and Interventions.* Chichester: Wiley & Sons.

Birchwood, M., Fowler, D. and Jackson, C. (2000) *Early Intervention in Psychosis: A Guide to Concepts, Evidence and Interventions.* Chichester: Wiley & Sons.

Birchwood, M., Mason, R., MacMillan, F. and Healy, J. (1993) 'Depression, Demoralisation and Control Over Psychotic Illness: A Comparison of Depressed and Non-Depressed Patients with a Chronic Psychosis.' *Psychological Medicine 23*, 387–395.

Blocher, D. (1983) 'Towards a Cognitive Developmental Approach to Counselling Supervision.' *Counselling Psychologist 11*, 27–34.

Bor, R., Gill, S., Miller, R. and Parrott, C. (2004) Doing Therapy Briefly. Basingstoke: Palgrave Macmillan.

Brewin, C. (1994) 'Changes in Attribution and Expressed Emotion in Relatives of Patients with Schizophrenia.' *Psychological Medicine 24*, 905–911.

Bridges, W. (2003) Managing Transitions (2nd edn). Cambridge, MA: Da Capo Press.

Brodoff, A. (1988) 'Schizophrenia through a Sister's Eyes: The Burden of Invisible Baggage.' *Schizophrenia Bulletin 14*, 1, 113–116.

Brooker, C. and Brabban, A. (2003) 'Implementing Evidence-Based Practice for People Who Experience Psychosis: Towards a Strategic Approach.' *Mental Health Review 8*, 2, 30–33.

Brooker, C. and Repper, J. (1998) *Serious Mental Health Problems in the Community – Policy, Practice and Research.* London: Bailliere Tindall.

Brown, G., Birley, J. and Wing, J. (1972) 'Influence of Family Life on the Course of Schizophrenia Disorders: A Replication.' *British Journal of Psychiatry 121*, 241–258.

Brown, G., Carstairs, G. and Topping, G. (1958) 'Post-Hospital Adjustment of Chronic Mental Patients.' *The Lancet 2*, 685–689.

Brown, G., Monck, E., Carstairs, G. and Wing, J. (1962) 'Influence of Family Life on the Course of Schizophrenic Illness.' *British Journal of Preventive and Social Medicine 16*, 55–68.

Budd, R. and Hughes, I. (1997) 'What do Relatives of People with Schizophrenia Find Helpful about Family Intervention?' *Schizophrenia Bulletin 23*, 2, 341–347.

Burbach, F. (1996) 'Family Based Interventions in Psychosis – An Overview and Comparison Between Family Therapy and Family Management Approaches.' *Journal of Mental Health 5*, 2, 111–134.

Burbach, F., Carter, J., Carter, J. and Carter, M. (2007) 'Assertive outreach and family work.' In R. Vellerman, E. Davis, G. Smith and M. Drage (eds) *Changing Outcomes in Psychosis.* Oxford: Blackwell Publishing.

Chadwick, P. (1997) *Schizophrenia: The Positive Perspective.* London: Routledge.

Chadwick, P., Birchwood, B. and Trower, P. (1996) *Evaluative Beliefs Scale. Cognitive Therapy for Delusions, Voices and Paranoia.* Chichester: Wiley & Sons.

Clarkson, P. (1995) *The Therapeutic Relationship.* London: Whurr.

Clements, K. and Turpin, G. (1992) 'Vulnerability Models and Schizophrenia: The Assessment and Prediction of Relapse.' In M. Birchwood and N. Tarrier *Innovations in the Psychological Management of Schizophrenia.* Chichester: Wiley & Sons.

Concise Oxford English Dictionary (1998) Oxford: Clarendon Press.

Corey, G. (1996) *Theory and Practice of Counselling and Psychotherapy* (5th edn). London: Brooks/Cole.

Creer, C. and Wing, J. (1974) *Schizophrenia at Home.* Surbiton: National Schizophrenia Fellowship.

Day, J., Wood, G., Dewey, M. and Bentall, P. (1995) 'A Self-Rating Scale for Measuring Neuroleptic Side-Effects.' *British Journal of Psychiatry 166,* 650–653.

Department of Health (1990a) *The Care Programme Approach for People with a Mental Illness Referred to the Specialist Psychiatric Services.* Department of Health Circular, HC(90)23/LASSL(90)11. London: HMSO.

Department of Health (1990b) *The Care Programme Approach for People with a Mental Illness Referred to the Specialist Psychiatric Services.* London: HMSO.

Department of Health (1995) *Building Bridges: A Guide to Arrangements for Inter-Agency Working for the Care and Protection of Severely Mentally Ill People.* London: HMSO.

Department of Health (1997) *The New NHS: Modern Dependable.* London: HMSO.

Department of Health (1999) *National Service Framework for Mental Health.* London: The Stationery Office.

Department of Health (2001) *Mental Health Policy Implementation Guideline.* London: The Stationery Office.

Department of Health. (2004) *The Ten Essential Shared Capabilities – A Framework for the Whole Mental Health Workforce.* London: Department of Health. Available at www.dh.gov.uk/publications.

Devane, S., Haddock, G., Lancashire, S, Baguley, I., *et al.* (1998) 'The Clinical Skills of Community Psychiatric Nurses Working with People who Have Severe and Enduring Mental Health Problems: An Empirical Analysis.' *Journal of Advanced Nursing 27,* 2, 253–260.

Dixon, L. and Lehman, A. (1995) 'Family Interventions for Schizophrenia.' *Schizophrenia Bulletin 21,* 423–441.

Drage, M., Floyd. S., Smith, G. and Cocks, N. (2004) *Evaluating Family Interventions: A Qualitative Investigation.* University of Bath: unpublished study.

Duncan, G., Sheitman, B. and Lieberman, J. (1999) 'An Integrated View of Pathophysiological Models of Schizophrenia.' *Brain Research Reviews 29,* 250–264.

Early Psychosis Prevention and Intervention Centre (1997) *Working with Family in Early Psychosis.* Melbourne: EPPIC. Available at www.eppic.org.au/.

Fadden, G. (1998) 'Family Intervention.' In C. Brooker and J. Repper (eds) *Serious Mental Health Problems in the Community – Policy, Practice and Research.* London: Bailliere Tindall.

Fadden, G., Bebbington, P. and Kuipers, E. (1987) 'The Burden of Care: The Impact of Functional Psychiatric Illness on the Patient's Family.' *British Journal of Psychiatry 150,* 285–292.

Falloon, I. and Shanahan, W. (1990) 'Community Management of Schizophrenia.' *British Journal of Hospital Medicine 443,* 62–66.

Falloon, I., Boyd, J. and McGill, C. (1984) *Family Care of Schizophrenia.* New York: Guildford Press.

Falloon, R., Laporta, M., Fadden, G. and Graham-Hole, V. (1993) *Managing Stress in Families. Cognitive and Behavioural Strategies for Enhancing Coping Skills.* London: Routledge.

Finkelman, A. (2000) 'Psychiatric Patients and Families: Moving from Catastrophic Event to Long-Term Coping.' *Home Care Provider*, August, 142–147.

Gamble, C. (2000) 'Using a Low Expressed Emotion Approach to Develop Positive Therapeutic Alliances.' In C. Gamble and G. Brennan (eds) *Working with Serious Mental Illness – A Practice Manual.* London: Bailliere Tindall.

Gamble, C. and Brennan, G. (2000) 'Working with Families and Informal Carers.' In C. Gamble and G. Brennan (eds) *Working with Serious Mental Illness – A Practice Manual.* London: Bailliere Tindall.

Gamble, C. and Midence, K. (1994) 'Schizophrenia Family Work: Mental Health Nurses Delivering an Innovative Service.' *Journal of Psychosocial Nursing 32*, 10, 13–16.

Glick, I.D., Clarkin, J.F., Haas, G.L. and Spencer Jr., J.H. (1993) 'Clinical Significance of Inpatient Family Intervention: Conclusions From a Clinical Trial.' *Hospital Community Psychiatry 44*, 9, 869–873.

Goffman, E. (1968) *Stigma.* Harmondsworth: Penguin Books Ltd.

Goldberg, D. and Williams, P. (1988) *A User's Guide to the General Health Questionnaire.* Windsor: NFER-Nelson.

Goldstein, M., Rodnick, E. and Evans, J. (1978) 'Drug and Family Therapy in the Aftercare of Acute Schizophrenia.' *Archives of General Psychiatry 35*, 1169–1177.

Grad, J. and Sainsbury, P. (1963) 'Mental Illness and the Family.' *The Lancet*, March, 544–547.

Gray, R. (2002) 'Medication Management for People with a Diagnosis of Schizophrenia.' *Nursing Times 98*, 47, 38–40.

Gregory, K. (2001) 'Integrating Counselling Within the Mental Health Services.' In K. Etherington (ed) *Counselling in Health Settings.* London: Jessica Kingsley Publishers.

Guttman, H. (1981) 'Systems Theory, Cybernetics and Epistemology.' In A. Gurman and D. Kniskern (eds) *Handbook of Family Therapy.* New York: Brunner/Mazel.

Harrison, P. (1999) 'Neurochemical Alterations in Schizophrenia Affecting the Putative Targets of Atypical Antipsychotics: Focus on Dopamine (D1, D2, D4) and 5HT 2A Receptors.' *British Journal of Psychiatry 174* (suppl. 38), 41–51.

Hatfield, A. (1997) 'Working Collaboratively with Families.' *Social Work in Mental Health: Trends and Issues 25*, 3, 77–85.

Hawkins, P. and Shohet, R. (2006) *Supervision in the Helping Professions* (3rd edn). Milton Keynes: Open University Press.

Heider, F. (1958) *The Psychology of Interpersonal Relations.* New York: Wiley.

Hewstone, M. and Stroebe, W. (eds) (2001) *Introduction to Social Psychology.* Oxford: Blackwell.

Hirsch, S. and Leff, J. (1975) *Abnormalities in Parents of Schizophrenics. Maudsley Monographs 22.* London: Oxford University Press.

Hoenig, J. and Hamilton, M. (1966) 'The Schizophrenic Patient and his Effect on the Household.' *International Journal of Social Psychiatry 12*, 165–176.

Hogan, T.P., Awad, A.G. and Eastwood, R. (1983) 'A Self Report Scale Predictive of Drug Compliance in Schizophrenics.' *Psychological Medicine 13*, 177–183.

Johnstone, L. (1993) 'Family Management in "Schizophrenia": Its Assumptions and Contradictions.' *Journal of Mental Health 2*, 255–269.

Jones, E.E. and Harris, V.A. (1967) 'The attribution of attitudes.' *Journal of Experimental Social Psychology 3*, 1–24.

Kane, J. (1989) 'The Current Status of Neuroleptics.' *Journal of Clinical Psychiatry 50*, 322–328.

Karp, D. and Tanarugsachock, V. (2000) 'Mental Illness, Caregiving and Emotional Management.' *Qualitative Health Research 10*, 1, 6–25.

Kasanin, J., Knight, E. and Sage, P. (1934) (cited in Brown, G., Monck, E., Carstairs, G. and Wing, J. (1962)) 'Influence of Family Life on the Course of Schizophrenic Illness.' *British Journal of Preventive and Social Medicine 16*, 55–68.

Kelley, H. (1967) 'Attribution in Social Psychology.' *Nebraska Symposium on Motivation 15*, 192–238.

Kellner, R. and Sheffield, B. (1973) 'A Self-Rating Scale of Distress.' *Psychological Medicine 3*, 88–100.

Kipling, R. (2000) *Just So Stories.* London: Penguin Books.

Krawiecka, M., Goldberg, D. and Vaughn, M. (1977) 'A Standardised Psychiatric Assessment Scale for Rating Chronic Psychotic Patients.' *Acta Psychiatrica Scandinavia 55*, 299–308.

Kuipers, E. and Raune, D. (2000) 'The Early Detection of Expressed Emotion and Burden in Families of First-Onset Psychosis.' In M. Birchwood, D. Fowler and C. Jackson (eds) *Early Intervention in Psychosis A Guide to Concepts, Evidence and Interventions.* Chichester: Wiley & Sons.

Kuipers, L., Leff, J. and Lam, D. (2002) *Family Work for Schizophrenia. A Practical Guide* (2nd edn). London: Gaskell.

Lafond, V. (1998) 'The Grief of Mental Illness: Context for the Cognitive Therapy of Schizophrenia.' In C. Perris and P. McGorry (eds) *Cognitive Psychotherapy of Psychotic and Personality Disorders: Handbook of Theory and Practice.* Chichester: Wiley & Sons.

Lafond, V. (2002) *Grieving Mental Illness* (2nd edn). Toronto: University of Toronto Press.

Laing, R. and Esterson, D. (1964) *Sanity, Madness and the Family.* London: Tavistock.

Lam, D. (1991) 'Psychosocial Family Interventions in Schizophrenia: A Review of Empirical Studies.' *Psychological Medicine 21*, 423–441.

Lancashire, S. (1998) 'The KGV (M) Symptom Scale Version 6.' University of Manchester: unpublished paper.

Leff, J. (1994) 'Working with the Families of Schizophrenic Patients.' *British Journal of Psychiatry 164* (suppl. 23), 71–76.

Leff, J. (1998) 'Needs of the Families of People with Schizophrenia.' *Advances in Psychiatric Treatment 4*, 277–284.

Leff, J. (2001) *The Unbalanced Mind.* London: Weidenfeld & Nicolson.

Leff, J. and Vaughn, C. (1985) *Expressed Emotion in Families.* New York: Guildford Press.

Leff, J., Kuipers, L., Berkowitz, R. and Sturgeon, D. (1985) 'A Controlled Trial of Social Intervention in the Families of Schizophrenic Patients: Two Year Follow-up.' *British Journal of Psychiatry 146*, 594–600.

Leff, J., Kuipers, L., Berkowitz, R., Eberlein-Vries, R. and Sturgeon, D. (1982) 'A Controlled Trial of Social Intervention in the Families of Schizophrenic Patients.' *British Journal of Psychiatry 141*, 121–134.

Leff, J., Sharpley, M., Chisholm, D., Bell, R. and Gamble, C. (2001) 'Training Community Psychiatric Nurses in Schizophrenia Family Work: A Study of Clinical and Economic Outcomes for Patients and Relatives.' *Journal of Mental Health 10*, 2, 189–197.

Lefley, H. (1996) *Family Caregiving in Mental Illness.* London: Sage Publications.

Lefley, H. and Johnson, D. (1990) *Families as Allies in Treatment of the Mentally Ill.* Washington: American Psychiatric Press.

Lelliot, P., Beevor, A., Hogman, G., Hislop, J., Lathean, J. and Ward, M. (2001) 'Carers' and Users' Expectations of Services – Carers Version.' *British Journal of Psychiatry 179*, 67–72.

Liese, B. and Beck, J. (1997) 'Cognitive Therapy Supervision.' In E. Watkins (ed) *Handbook of Clinical Supervision.* New York: John Wiley & Sons.

Linszen, D., Dingemans, P., Van Der Does, J., Nugter, A. *et al.* (1996) 'Treatment, Expressed Emotion and Relapse in Recent Onset Schizophrenic Disorders.' *Psychological Medicine 26*, 333–342.

Macmillan, F. and Shiers, D. (2000) 'The IRIS Programme.' In M. Birchwood, D Fowler and C. Jackson (eds) *Early Intervention in Psychosis. A Guide to Concepts, Evidence and Interventions.* Chichester: Wiley.

Mari, J. and Streiner, D. (1994) 'An Overview of Family Interventions and Relapse on Schizophrenia: A Meta-Analysis of Research Findings.' *Psychological Medicine 24, 3*, 565–578.

Marsh, D., Lefley, H., Evans-Rhodes, D., Ansell, V. *et al.* (1996) 'The Experience of Mental Illness: Evidence for Resilience.' *Psychiatric Rehabilitation Journal 20, 2*, 3–12.

McCann, E. and Bowers, L. (2005) 'Training in Cognitive Behavioural Interventions on Acute Psychiatric Wards.' *Journal of Psychiatric and Mental Health Nursing 12*, 215–222.

McCann, G., McKeown, M. and Porter, I. (1996) 'Understanding the Needs of Relatives Within a Special Hospital for Mentally Disordered Offenders: A Basis for Improved Services.' *Journal of Advanced Nursing 23*, 346–352.

McFarlane, W. (1994) 'Multiple-Family Groups and Psychoeducation in the Treatment of Schizophrenia.' *New Directions for Mental Health Services 62*, 13–22.

McFarlane, W. (2000) 'Psychoeducational Multi-Family Groups.' In B. Martindale, A. Bateman, M. Crowe and F. Margison (eds) *Psychosis – Psychological Approaches and their Effectiveness.* London: Gaskell.

McFarlane, W., Luckens, E., Link, B., Dushay, R. *et al.* (1995) 'The Multiple Family Group, Psychoeducation, and Maintenance Medication in the Treatment of Schizophrenia.' *Archives of General Psychiatry 52*, 679–687.

McGoldrich, M., Gerson, R. and Shellenberger, S. (1999) *Genograms: Assessment and Intervention.* London: Norton & Co. Ltd.

McGuffin, P., Farmer, A. and Gottesman, I. (1987) 'Is There Really a Split in Schizophrenia? The Genetic Evidence.' *British Journal of Psychiatry 150*, 581–592.

Mehta, S. and Farina, A. (1997) 'Is Being "Sick" Really Better? Effect of the Disease View of Mental Disorder on Stigma.' *Journal of Social and Clinical Psychology 16*, p.405–419.

Miklowitz, D. and Goldstein, M. (1997) *Bipolar Disorder. A Family-Focused Treatment Approach.* London: The Guilford Press.

Miller, F. (1996) 'Grief Therapy for Relatives of Persons with Serious Mental Illness.' *Psychiatric Services 47*, 633–637.

Miller, F., Dworkin, J., Ward, M. and Barone, D. (1990) 'A Preliminary Study of Unresolved Grief in Families of Seriously Mentally Ill Patients.' *Hospital and Community Psychiatry 12*, 1321–1325.

Miller, W. and Rollnick, S. (1991) *Motivational Interviewing. Preparing People to Change Addictive Behaviour.* London: Guilford Press.

Miller, W. and Rollnick, S. (2002) *Motivational Interviewing. Preparing People to Change Addictive Behaviour* (2nd edn) London: Guilford Press.

Milne, D. and James, I. (2000) 'A Systematic Review of Effective Cognitive Behavioural Supervision.' *British Journal of Clinical Psychology 39*, 111–127.

Mistral, W., Drage, M., Smith, G., Floyd, F. and Cocks, N. (2007) 'Carer-Practitioner Collaboration in Research and Evaluation.' In R. Vellerman, E. Davis, G. Smith and M. Drage (eds) *Changing Outcomes in Psychosis.* Oxford: Blackwell Publishing.

Mohr, W., Lafuze, J. and Mohr, B. (2000) 'Opening Caregiver Minds: National Alliance for the Mentally Ill's Provider Education Program.' *Archives of Psychiatric Nursing 14*, 5, 235–243.

Moore, E., Ball, R. and Kuipers, E. (1992) 'Expressed Emotion in Staff Working with the Long-Term Mentally Ill.' *British Journal of Psychiatry 161*, 802–808.

National Institute for Clinical Excellence (2002) *Core Interventions in the Treatment and Management of Schizophrenia in Primary and Secondary Care. Clinical Guideline.* London: National Institute for Clinical Excellence.

Nuechterlein, K. (1987) 'Vulnerability Models: State of the Art.' In H. Hafner, W. Gattaz and W. Jangerik (eds) *Searches for the Cause of Schizophrenia.* Berlin: Springer-Verlag.

Nuechterlein, K. and Subotnik, K. (1998) 'The Cognitive Origins of Schizophrenia and Prospects for Intervention.' In T. Wykes, N. Tarrier and S. Lewis (eds) *Outcome and Innovation in Psychological Treatment of Schizophrenia.* Chichester: Wiley & Sons.

Ostman, M. and Kjellin, L. (2002) 'Stigma by Association.' *British Journal of Psychiatry 181*, 494–498.

Overall, J. and Gorham, D. (1962) 'The Brief Psychiatric Rating Scale.' *Psychological Reports 10*, 799–812.

Parkes, C. M. (1998) *Bereavement: Studies of Grief in Adult Life.* London: Pelican.

Patterson, P., Birchwood, M. and Cochrane, R. (2000) 'Preventing the Entrenchment of High Expressed Emotion in First Episode Psychosis: Early Developmental Attachment Pathways.' *Australian and New Zealand Journal of Psychiatry 34* (suppl.) S191–S197.

Pearlin, L. and Schooler, C. (1978) 'The Structure of Coping.' *Journal of Health and Science Behavior 19*, 2–12.

Penn, D., Guynan, K., Daily, T., Spaulding W., Garbin, C. and Sullivan, M. (1994) 'Dispelling the Stigma of Schizophrenia: What Sort of Information is Best?' *Schizophrenia Bulletin 20*, 3, 567–578.

Pharoah, F., Rathbone. J., Mari, J. and Streiner, D. (2005) *Family Intervention for Schizophrenia (Review).* The Cochrane Library, Issue 4. West Sussex: Wiley Press.

Pitschel-Walz, G., Leucht, S., Bauml, J., Kissling, W. and Engel, R. (2001) 'The Effect of Family Interventions on Relapse and Rehospitalisation in Schizophrenia: A Meta-Analysis.' *Schizophrenia Bulletin 27*, 1, 73–92.

Platt, S. (1985) 'Measuring the Burden of Psychiatric Illness on the Family: An Evaluation of Some Rating Scales.' *Psychological Medicine 15*, 383–393.

Porter, S. (1996) 'Qualitative Research.' In D. Cormack (ed) *The Research Process in Nursing* (3rd edn). Oxford: Blackwell Science.

Priebe, S., Huxley, P., Knight, S. and Evans, S. (1999) 'Application of the Manchester Short Assessment of Quality of Life (MANSA).' *International Journal of Social Psychiatry 45*, 1, 7–12.

Read, J. (2002) 'The Need for Evidence Based Destigmatization Programmes.' *ISPS Newsletter 5*, 2, 16–22.

Repper, J. and Perkins, R. (1996) *Working Alongside People with Long Term Mental Health Problems.* London: Chapman & Hall.

Repper, J. and Perkins, R. (2003) *Social Inclusion and Recovery.* Edinburgh: Bailliere Tindall.

Rogers, C. and Stevens, B. (1967) *Person to Person. The Problem of Being Human.* London: Souvenir Press.

Sainsbury Centre for Mental Health (1998) *Keys to Engagement.* London: SCMH.

Sainsbury Centre for Mental Health (2003) *A Window of Opportunity.* London: SCMH.

Scazufca, M. and Kuipers, E. (1996) 'Links Between Expressed Emotion and Burden of Care in Relatives of Patients with Schizophrenia.' *British Journal of Psychiatry 168*, 580–587.

Schene, A., Tessler, R. and Gamache, G. (1996) 'Care-Giving in Serious Mental Illness: Conceptualization and Measurement.' In H. Kindsworth and G. Thornicroft (eds) *Health Service Evaluation.* Cambridge: Cambridge University Press.

Smith, G. (1999) 'Linking Theory with Practice.' *Mental Health Care 3*, 4, 133–135.

Smith, G. (2003) 'An Exploration of Experiences and Coping Responses of Parents of Forensic Schizophrenia Patients.' University of Manchester: unpublished dissertation.

Smith, G. and Velleman, R. (2002) 'Maintaining a Family Work for Psychosis Service by Recognising and Addressing the Barriers to Implementation.' *Journal of Mental Health 11*, 5, 471–479.

Smith, G., Drage, M., Drage, A., Drage, J. and Drage, E. (in press) Positive Risk-Taking.

Smith, J. (2000) *Early Warning Signs. A Self Management Training Manual for Individuals with Psychosis.* Worcestershire Community and Mental Health Trust.

Spencer, E., Murray, E. and Plaistow, J. (2000) 'Relapse Prevention in Early Psychosis.' In M. Birchwood, D. Fowler and C. Jackson (eds) *Early Intervention in Psychosis. A Guide to Concepts, Evidence and Interventions.* Chichester: Wiley & Sons.

Szmuckler, G., Burgess, P., Hermann, H., Benson, A., Colusa, S. and Block, S. (1996) 'Caring for a Relative with Serious Mental Illness: The Development of the Experience of Caregiving Inventory.' *Society for Psychiatry and Psychiatric Epidemiology 31*, 137–148.

Tarrier, N., Barrowclough, C., Porceddu, K. and Fitzpatrick, E. (1994) 'The Salford Intervention Project: Relapse Rates at Five and Eight Years.' *British Journal of Psychiatry 153*, 532–542.

Tarrier, N., Barrowclough, C., Vaughn, C., Bamrah, J. *et al.* (1988) 'The Community Management of Schizophrenia: A Controlled Trial of Behavioural Intervention to Reduce Relapse.' *British Journal of Psychiatry 165*, 829–832.

Thompson, S. (2005) 'Food for Thought.' *Mental Health Practice 9*, 4, 47.

Torrey, E., Taylor, E., Bracha, H., Bowler, A. *et al.* (1994) 'Prenatal Origin of Schizophrenia in a Sub-Group of Discordant Monozygotic Twins.' *Schizophrenia Bulletin 20*, 423–432.

Vaughan, K., Doyle, M., McConaughy, N., Blaszaynski, A., Fox, A. and Tarrier, N. (1992) 'The Sydney Intervention Trial: A Controlled Trial of Relatives Counseling to Reduce Schizophrenic Relapse.' *Social Psychiatry and Psychiatric Epidemiology 26*, 16–21.

Vellerman, R., Davis, E., Smith, G. and Drage, M. (2007) *Changing Outcomes in Psychosis.* Oxford: Blackwell Publishing.

Venables, P. and Wing, J. (1962) 'Levels of Arousal and the Subclassification of Schizophrenia.' *Archives of General Psychiatry 7*, 114–119.

Von Bertalanffy, L. (1968) *General Systems Theory: Foundations, Development, Applications.* New York: George Braziller.

Wahl, O. and Harman, C. (1989) 'Family Views of Stigma.' *Schizophrenia Bulletin 15*, 1, 131–139.

Webb, C., Pfeiffer, M., Mueser, K., Gladis, M. *et al.* 'Burden and Well-Being of Caregivers for the Severely Mentally Ill: The Role of Coping Style and Social Style.' *Schizophrenia Research 34*, 169–180.

Willetts, L. and Leff, J. (1997) 'Expressed Emotion and Schizophrenia: The Efficacy of a Staff Training Programme.' *Journal of Advanced Nursing 26*, 1125–1133.

Winefield, H. and Burnett, P. (1996) 'Barriers to an Alliance Between Family and Professional Caregivers in Chronic Schizophrenia.' *Journal of Mental Health 5*, 3, 223–232.

Wing, J. and Brown, G. (1970) *Institutionalism and Schizophrenia.* Cambridge: Cambridge University Press.

World Health Organization (1979) *International Pilot Study of Schizophrenia.* Chichester: Wiley & Son.

World Health Organization (2004) *Early Psychosis Declaration.* Geneva: World Health Organization.

Wright, H. (1989) *Group Work Perspectives and Practice for Nurses.* Harrow: Scutari Press.

Wykes, T., Tarrier, N. and Lewis, S. (1998) *Outcome and Innovation in Psychological Treatment of Schizophrenia.* Chichester: Wiley & Sons.

Zastowny, T., Lehman, A., Cole, R. and Kane, C. (1992) 'Family Management of Schizophrenia: A Comparison of Behavioural and Supportive Family Treatment.' *Psychiatric Quarterly 62*, 2, 159–186.

Zubin, J. and Spring, B. (1977) 'Vulnerability: A New View of Schizophrenia.' *Journal of Abnormal Psychology 86*, 103–126.

Subject Index

Author Index